Theology Today
37 Theology of Mission

Theology Today

GENERAL EDITOR:
EDWARD YARNOLD, S.J.

No. 37

Theology of Mission

BY

AYLWARD SHORTER, W.F.

THE MERCIER PRESS,
4, BRIDGE STREET, CORK

FOR
NJELU

Nihil Obstat:
Jeremiah J. O'Sullivan, D.D.
Censor deputatus
28 January 1972

Imprimatur:
Cornelius Ep. Corag. & Ross
18 July 1972

SBN 85342 299 0

ACKNOWLEDGEMENTS

The scriptural quotations are given according to *The Jerusalem Bible,* which is © 1966, 1967, 1968 by Darton, Longman and Todd Ltd. and Doubleday & Co. Inc., and is used by kind permission of the publishers.

Quotations from *The Documents of Vatican II* (ed. W. M. Abbott, S.J.) are printed by kind permission of the America Press and Geoffrey Chapman, Ltd., London. The documents are referred to by the following titles:

Ad Gentes: Decree on the Church's Missionary Activity.
Nostra Aetate: Declaration on the Relationship of the Church to non-Christian Religions.
Gaudium et Spes: Pastoral Constitution on the Church in the Modern World.

CONTENTS

THE AUTHOR

After serving in the King's African Rifles in East Africa, Aylward Shorter studied Modern History at The Queen's College, Oxford, and then joined the White Fathers. He was ordained in 1962. He then studied Missiology at the Gregorianum in Rome, and took the Diploma in Social Anthropology at Oxford. For two years he undertook field research in Tanzania for a D. Phil. thesis at Oxford. This was completed in 1968. Since then he has been teaching at The Pastoral Institute of Eastern Africa, Gaba, and – part-time – in the Department of Sociology, Makerere University, Kampala.

PREFACE

It is not all that many years since a Catholic historian wrote that 'Europe is the faith and the faith is Europe'. It is very few years since a writer in a missionary magazine rejoiced in the fact that everywhere he moved in Nigeria he felt the spirit of Ireland.

These remarks contain at least two false presuppositions. The first is that there is an ideal Christian culture, so that a missionary can convert people in 'missionary countries' to the faith only by converting them to the western culture in which the missionary himself experiences the faith. The second false presupposition is that the Church's missionary activity is only directed towards non-western cultures.

On the contrary, there is no specifically Christian culture. The Church's mission is to proclaim Christ to all nations of every culture, eastern or western, so that Christianity can be authentically embodied in terms of that culture. This is the theme of Fr Shorter's book.

E. J. Yarnold, S.J.

FOREWORD

This is a personal book, but not an original one, as might be expected from an author who is an anthropologist, and not a professional theologian. It is the fruit of a certain amount of undisciplined reading, most of which is acknowledged either in the text or in the bibliography at the end of the book. However, it is much more the fruit of discussion with visitors to The Pastoral Institute at Gaba over the past three years. These have included Fr Adrian Hastings, Fr J. Donders W.F., Fr A. Nebreda S.J., Fr H. van Pinksteren M.H.M., Professor John Mbiti, Fr B. Joinet W.F., Fr H. Horan W.F., Fr A. M. Lugira, and Professor Bernard Cooke. Members of the Institute's staff have also helped consciously or unconsciously in the writing of the book, in particular, Fr. G. Heuthorst M.H.M., Mgr Pierre Riches and Sister Josephine Lucker M.M. Finally, I owe a very great deal to my students with many of whom I have discussed the ideas in this book either singly or collectively, and some of whom have read over the typescript. To all these friends and collaborators I owe a debt of thanks.

If the reader finds too many references to Africa, this is because I am a missionary of Africa and my interests are primarily African. I apologize for this bias.

Lastly, a word about my application of Senghor's word 'Super-Person' to Christ in Chapter Six. Some of those who read the typescript took objection to this word, since it smacked of 'Superman' and this could suggest to some that Christ was superhuman. I have no wish to suggest that Christ's human nature is in any way different from our own, even though he is more human than any of us. However, I have retained the world Senghor coined, because, besides being the obvious application of his theory of socialization, it is also strictly true that Christ is a divine, and not a human, person.

Aylward Shorter W.F.
The Pastoral Institute of Eastern Africa,
Gaba, Kampala, Uganda. September 1970.

CHAPTER 1

Development, the New Name of Mission?

Pope Paul VI landed at Entebbe, Uganda, on the last day of July 1969, the first reigning Pope to set foot on African soil. The speech he made on arrival contained one very striking statement. 'Development', he said, 'is the new name of Peace.' In fact the subject of development and the Church's co-operation in government programmes of development was a major theme of the Pope's nineteen addresses and speeches during his three day visit to Africa. How far was the Pope's preoccupation with problems of development an echo of a new interest in the Church, an interest accompanied by a corresponding lack of interest in what used to be regarded as the proper task of the missionary – the preaching to, and conversion of, the non-Christian? Missiologists lament sometimes the drop in the number of missionary vocations. But there is a boom in the membership of volunteer organizations. Missionaries complain that they cannot obtain funds for pastoral needs, but they are readily available for social or material development. Expatriates are viewed with suspicion by governments unless they are fully committed to socio-economic development. The words mission and missionary have become almost synonyms for bigotry, detachment and self-interest, and the author of a book on *The Theology of Mission* has to ask himself whether a better title might not be *The Theology of Development*. Should not the Pope have said: 'Development is the new name of Mission'? The answer must depend on the stage of evolution reached by Mission Theology. If the question is to be more than merely cynical, and if the equation between Mission and Development can be seriously made, then the terms of the equation must be rendered sufficiently broad. At the popular level the ideas of Mission and Development are too narrow to admit of their being interchanged in the title of a book like this, but it is the contention of the author that Mission Theology is moving already in this direction and that new conceptions of Mission and Development are gaining ground among theologians. It must not be thought, however, that professional theologians are capable of suddenly bestowing a new theological dimension upon the Church. They are merely a part of the process by which the whole People of God becomes aware of the voice of the Holy Spirit. If a new dimension in Mission Theology is being given to us, it must be that, in the contemporary situation, the old idea of Mission has been found unsatisfactory. The missionary crisis turns out, in fact, to be the crisis of an outmoded ideal, and if Christians today do not want to be missionaries, it may be that they have come to a better understanding of the missionary ideal, rather than that they have no missionary ideal at all.

Chesterton once told the story of a farm boy whose cottage stood on the slope of one of the great Wessex hills. The boy had never left home, but one day he set out on his travels to look for one of those giant effigies which are found scrawled on the flanks of hills. When he was far away he looked back to see his family homestead and to his amazement saw that his own home was standing in the middle of just such a white horse or effigy. He had always lived in the midst of that giant figure, but it had been too large and too close to be seen. Now, however, that he had left home, he was able to see it for the first time. Something like that has happened to the Church's understanding of its mission as a result of the enormous missionary expansion which has taken place over the last century. Until that expansion took place, 'Europe was the Faith'. The majority of Christians lived in Europe and the Western world influenced by Europe. The resources in materials and personnel lay in the West. Above all, Theology – even Mission Theology – was written in the West. Much of all this is still true today, but the picture is already changing. In order to understand its mission, the Church had to become practically and effectively missionary. This it did between the years 1869 and 1962.

At the First Vatican Council a tiny fraction of the 700 Bishops and Prelates who took part had come from the so-called mission countries. At Vatican II more than one third of the 2,500 Bishops and Prelates came from mission countries, and 170 of them were natives of Asia and Africa. Vatican II was the first missionary council of the Church. For the first time a council of the Church was not a council of Christendom alone. The two billion non-Christians of the world were represented through the pastors of mission dioceses, and their presence alone was enough to help the Council see the Church in its true perspective. Like the farm boy in Chesterton's parable, the Church suddenly discovered the true and total context of its hitherto sheltered life. That context was the world. The Church's task is to speak to the world with the voice of Christ – to be the 'Sacrament of the World', a sign and instrument of the unity of mankind in God through Christ. The task of the Church does not end with a self-servicing in-group of baptized believers. It does not concentrate exclusively on those areas where Christianity can acquire a privileged position and become the established religion of a particular culture. The Second Vatican Council put a stop to the search for the chimera called Christendom. After the Council the Church is a Diaspora, living not for itself but – like its founder – for others. A man is baptized, not for his own salvation alone, but for the mission to the world since it is only through that mission that he can be one with Christ whose mission it is. His likeness to Christ consists in being 'a man for others'.

Some missiologists persist in seeing an opposition between the pastoral and missionary functions of the Church, and this is a product of pre-conciliar thinking. Although one must still discuss the important question of priorities in the Church, no opposition can be brought between the Church and her 'missions'. It will be one of the arguments of this book that the question of priorities can only be solved when Church and Mission are identified. The 'missions' are not 'foreign missions' – an extraneous phenomenon, an abnormal and highly temporary situation in the Church, tolerated because it is a necessary prelude to the establishment of a universal and 'once and for all' Christian Civilization. The Church's mission, and therefore her 'missions', are of her very essence. She must always confront mankind and the world as long as the world exists. Her mission is never over. In a sense, it is only when the Church is mature and has become a factor of positive relevance to a given human society, that its mission has begun. It certainly does not stop at that moment, and become a 'pastoral', self-servicing activity.

It would, perhaps, be too much to say that this view of the Church's mission reigns unchallenged, but there are clear signs that theological thinking is going in this direction. At the Second Vatican Council a number of missionary bishops actually attempted to prevent the discussion and promulgation of a decree on the missions. They wanted no discussion of the missions apart from that of mission in the Constitution on the Church. In the event, however, the distinction between Church and Missions was canonized by the promulgation of two conciliar documents on these subjects, even though the second can only be understood with reference to the first. A very good index to the progress of missiological thinking is to compare the titles of works of missiology over the past thirty years: *Missions and Missionaries* (1932); *Worship, the Life of the Missions* (1958); *Liturgy and the Missions* (1960); *Christian Missions and Social Ferment* (1964); *A History of Christian Missions* (1964); *The World Mission of the Church* (1964); *The Church as Mission* (1966); *Church and Mission in Modern Africa* (1967); *Missions and Religions* (1968); *The Church is Mission* (1969). There is a clear progress from Missions to Mission, and a progress in the degree of association of Mission with the Church itself.

When Pope Paul said that development is the new name of peace, he was already subscribing to a wider notion of development than mere economics. Peace is not the mere absence of war. It is the active principle of harmony between individuals and groups of individuals. Therefore it must include justice and the will to help one another achieve a suitable level of material prosperity and, above all, human dignity. Cold war is not peace, even though the parties may be bound together by economic ties of investment and trade. If development means peace, it demands a certain amount of altruism, an altruism that is not satisfied with the limitations set by the profit motive and the law of competition. More than this, development must rise above the sphere of economics itself. It must be a complete and integral development of the whole man. Development is nothing if it is not human, if it does not aim at the personal and cultural fulfilment of man. *Homo Economicus* was long ago discovered by social anthropologists to be a fiction, and one of the themes of this book is that human personality is, to an important extent, a cultural personality.

Increasingly missionaries tend to be ashamed of the specifically Christian aspects of their mission. Increasingly they tend to see themselves as secular governments often see them – voluntary agencies contributing to the socio-economic development of the people they serve. A missionary like Father John J. Considine is able to write a book which deals exclusively with the ways and means of making the missionary more effective in his contribution to socio-economic betterment. Such handbooks are extremely practical, but they do not provide any justification for the missionary's involvement in such work. Is the Church in a mission territory merely a channel for the deployment of the Vatican's material resources, the parallel of organizations set up by secular governments for giving aid to developing countries? That is how the governments of these countries see the Church, and if they see it in this way it must be because the Church herself has failed to convince them that her spiritual message is bound up with the process of development. For these governments socio-economic betterment is the final aim. Religious allegiances and divisions are obstacles to the achievement of this aim, obstacles which must be played down at all costs in the interests of national unity and material progress. The Church does not believe that the human spirit can be harnessed to so low an ideal. It believes that human development demands a degree of freedom and autonomy in the spiritual sphere which entails diversity and the respect for diversity. If development is peace, it is the truly Catholic ideal of respecting and promoting the vision and values in each other's cultural and religious traditions. It is listening as much as speaking – a dialogue and not a double monologue.

Theologians can look at development from different points of view. From one angle development can be seen negatively as the progressive liberation from evils of various kinds, especially from the classic evils of poverty, ignorance and disease. Development is thus a continual emancipation, but, as the theologians point out, it is not an emancipation from purely material or physical evils. Man must be emancipated from his own evil tendencies, his own passions. He must be emancipated from social tensions, from cultural arrogance. He may not even be aware of the chains that bind him. Often they are invisible chains, but he learns of their existence through religious faith, and this learned faith enables him to attain an even higher level of freedom and assurance. Since Body and Spirit are not separable and our spirit expresses itself in a bodily fashion, the Church's role is to liberate men bodily as well as spiritually. In fact, it cannot liberate men spiritually, if it does not also do so bodily, but the danger lies in seeing only the body. Without faith the liberation cannot become spiritual.

From another angle development can be seen positively as the progressive domination, or humanization, by man of the world. Man is continuing the process of creation begun by God, obeying the Creator's command to go forth, dominate and subdue the earth. This approach affords us a theology of work, a theology of terrestrial realities, a theology of secular culture, but once again it must go further than the visible and the tangible. To achieve this goal of humanization, man must himself be human. He must perfect and live to the full his humanity. Christian faith enables him to do this at both the personal and cultural level through his experimental knowledge of the risen Christ, located bodily and spatially in his fellow men. The Church does not necessarily ask secular governments to share her faith, not even to consider the claims she makes, but she does ask that the humanizing effects of faith be recognized, and, above all, that they depend upon the genuineness and spontaneity of that faith. In the interests of human development, therefore, the Church asks that her faith be safeguarded, even promoted. The Church presents herself to the secular government as a humanist desiring merely that her sincerity should go unquestioned when she says that only human values are Christian. As a humanist the Church's faith in man is unbounded. There are no limits to man's emancipation, no limits to his development because it is Christ who is the principle of this movement and its term. Christ is unbounded. In him there is no end to humanization and human development.

The rediscovery of the Church's mission at the Second Vatican Council was the rediscovery of the Church's human context, her world context. For this she cannot ever be grateful enough to the so-called mission countries. In giving the Church this vision the mission countries have given back to those countries where Christianity has been established for many centuries a return more precious than all the resources, human and material, that the western world has poured into South America, Africa and Asia. The Church's mission is at last seen as a two-way process, a genuine exchange between the different sections of humanity.

It is Christ who has revealed his Father to us and his gospel is the foundation of our theology. In Christ we understand the full meaning of mission and the full meaning of development. Mission and development meet and become one in Christ. This book must therefore be centred on Christ. Before considering the person of Christ, however, we must divest ourselves of any lingering preconceptions about the Church's mission. This we do in the next chapter. After that we shall examine the Old Testament in the light of Christ's own message to see how that message was prepared. We shall then consider the foundation of the Church's mission in the person of Christ and how Christ is the 'Glory of Man' in all that concerns material development, fulfilment of human personality, and the promotion of human culture. It will then be time to examine the essential connection between the Church's mission and her universality, and in what this universality consists. We must also discuss the continuity of the Church's mission. Finally, we shall say something about the Church's mission in relation to the problems of affluence and secularism, putting foward the proposition that the so-called mission countries have a contribution to make towards the solution of these problems.

CHAPTER 2

The Era of Foreign Missions

This chapter has to be a somewhat negative one. The intention is to present a picture of mission which was common before the Second Vatican Council, and if the picture is a trifle exaggerated it is more to highlight current emphases in mission theology than to debunk previous generations of theologians and missionaries. In any case, as everyone knows, all progress in knowledge proceeds from the mistakes of those who have gone before. There is nothing reprehensible in making mistakes, especially when – as was the case here – those who made them were sincerely seeking the answer to a difficult problem.

The origin of the Church as mission lies in the Godhead itself, in the Blessed Trinity. This was commonly taught before Vatican II, and it is taught no less today. However, there has been a shift in emphasis away from an extrinsic, juridical relationship, to a more intrinsic and vital one. The Son's mission comes from the Father, and the mission of the Holy Spirit comes from both Father and Son. The mission of the Apostles, 'the sent ones', it was said, took its origin from the command of Christ who sent them, and the mission of the Church today derives from the mission of the apostles. The Holy Spirit is not one of the senders of the apostles, but is himself sent with them to animate the Church.

The picture thus presented is one of a chain of command, analogous to the chain of command in military circles. Orders are transmitted from an order group at battalion level to successive order groups at company and platoon level, with the ever present risk that the commands will be distorted. The simultaneous mission of the Spirit with the apostles obviates this danger, and serves as a kind of guarantee of a direct link with the Trinity. In spite of this, the scheme tends to make the mission of the Church remote from the mission of the Son. The Church's mission was seen primarily as the fulfilment of a command issued many centuries ago.

The command was to teach and to baptize all nations and this was understood to mean the actual baptism of every indivual and the creation of homogeneous Christian nations. With this ideal in mind we prayed for 'the conversion of England' or 'the conversion of Africa'. Conversion was a numerical affair and numbers were an important index of evangelizing a nation. Success was reported by counting visible things such as numbers of baptisms, numbers of confessions, numbers of communions. One day every human being would either be a Christian or have had the chance to become one, and the Church would then be truly and effectively Catholic. Until that day dawned evangelization was a piecemeal process. Some countries would be fully fledged Christian nations, with Christianity the established religion and, possibly, a Concordat signed with the Holy See, others would scarcely have a church at all. The Church was in the process of being founded in these countries. These were the missions – the foreign missions, an abnormal state of affairs that demanded abnormal policies and structures. The foreignness of the missions even found expression in the abnormal appearance of the missionaries who wore long beards, for example, when priests in the civilized world went clean shaven. Missionary regions had no bishops or dioceses. The Pope alone was bishop of the missions, and those who belonged to the episcopal order in the missions were his vicars. Because of the fewness of the missionaries, lay ministers had to be appointed as catechists, exercising pastoral functions usually reserved to the priest in Christian countries, such as preaching, leading public prayer, visiting, giving advice, helping the sick and dying and baptizing in cases of necessity. The catechumenate which had disappeared in the Western world since the days of the early Church was revived in the missions.

Although western Christians had unbounded admiration for the heroism and self-sacrifice of missionaries, they regarded their work with an amused tolerance. Missionaries were simple souls, who did not have to reflect very much about what they were doing. They were the shock troops of the Church who received their orders from the centre. Mission theology, mission policies, mission priorities were made or decided in Europe. The funds, too, came from Europe and the average western Christian felt he had satisfied his missionary obligations by putting money annually in a collection plate that was proffered to him by a bearded apparition in a large hat or a red fez. The only literature about the missions was sentimental or sensational – or even a little cynical – designed as it was to extract donations and not to inform people about missionary work.

If the missions made little impact on the western world, what kind of an impression was conveyed by the Church to the people in mission lands? Much depended on the attitude of the missionaries themselves. Broadly speaking, missionaries had a pessimistic and negative approach to all they found in mission countries. To begin with, no fine distinctions were drawn on the question of salvation outside the visible Church. In practice the people of mission lands were damned – in the grip of Satan himself. The members of one African missionary society, for example, used to recite every day a prayer to Our Lady which included the following petition: 'Have mercy on these unfortunate creatures [the Muslims and Infidels] who are continually falling into hell in spite of the merits of your Son, Jesus Christ.' Early missionaries saw the devil everywhere. Bishop Shanahan in Nigeria was personally convinced that the devil was physically preventing him from entering certain villages, and the hard beginnings of many a mission were attributed by missionaries to the personal intervention of Satan, reluctant to let African or Asian souls out of his clutches. In missionary eyes mission lands were the 'Empire of Satan'.

One of the consequences of this outlook was to stress the need for as many individual baptisms as possible, regardless of whether real Christian communities were being formed, or whether the newly baptized would have sufficient opportunity to practise their faith. The Church was an institution to provide baptism. What happened afterwards was not so important. Another consequence of this outlook was to reinforce the ghetto or fortress Church. The world was wholly evil, especially the pagan world, and the Church had to stand apart from the world, uncontaminated by it. Practical expression of this idea can still be seen in the great complexes of mission buildings that were put up. Missions were not built in the towns, or in any large concentration of populations. Amenities were clustered together, church, schools, hospitals, dispensaries, teacher-training centres, seminaries, printing-presses, workshops, co-operatives and agricultural schemes. The mission was a little 'colony' all on its own. It was a world apart from the village-world of the people. People came to the mission, not the mission to the people.

Living in a world apart, missionaries had small chance of sharing the social life of the people they evangelized. They were insulated against it, surrounded as they were by the familiar institutions of their European homelands, transplanted on to an alien soil, and by a legion of middlemen, catechists, teachers, and servants, always anxious to please their employers and blocking effective, sustained contact with the people. The missionaries were altogether too few to be able to dispense with such middlemen, but the concentration of resources and personnel often made them an obstacle to, as well as a vehicle of, communication.

Such physical disadvantages were largely of the missionaries' own making. Some early missionary strategists like Cardinal Lavigerie warned against the dangers of creating isolated Christian villages, and yet the warnings were unheeded and this is exactly what the missions in fact became. The easiest way to start a mission was to collect orphans or ransom slave-children and then start a mission school. This then developed into a Christian village on the model of the Jesuit 'Reductions' in South America, where the minutest detail in the lives of the inhabitants was regulated by the missionaries, and all obeyed the mission bell which summoned them to work, meals, sleep, recreation and prayer. In some cases the missionaries inherited a settlement of this kind from a colonial philanthropic society or merchant company, but however the great, paternalistic mission complexes arose, the net result was always the same; the missionaries were not permeating a society which already existed with its own human values and traditions, so much as creating their own type of society artificially.

Not of their own making was the antecedent ignorance of the missionaries about the cultures to which they came. The world to which they came was an unknown world and the scientific disciplines destined to study this world were still in their infancy. Sociology and Social Anthropology barely existed. Even so, missionaries were suspicious of secular learning and much of this learning was deliberately hostile to the ideals and aims of a missionary Church, if not to religion itself. Missionaries themselves played a large part in developing these sciences and applying them to the social phenomena of hitherto unknown peoples, but in the early days they were necessarily ignorant and their first instinct was to mistrust what they did not know or understand. Mistrust was bad enough, but the mission theology of the time made missionaries despise non-Christian cultures, and such contempt could look dangerously like a sense of racial superiority.

Contempt took many forms. It was directed at non-Christian beliefs, morals, art and social practices. At worst, primitive man was worshipping the devil; at best he was practising superstition. He was guided in his conduct by nothing but his instincts and propensities, and governed by unchecked passion. His music and art was crude and barbaric. A missionary described his own immediate task in the following words: 'We teach lawless men to become obedient, inhuman men to love, savage men to change.' Another father reported with approval an African's reaction to the suggestion that one day there would be African priests: 'You can as soon tame a lion, as make an African a priest.' As non-Christian peoples came to be better known, the pendulum began to swing in the opposite direction. Under the influence of Max Muller, Andrew Lang and the Vienna School of Father Wilhelm Schmidt, S.V.D., a more optimistic view began to be taken of non-Christian religions, but the new attitude did no more justice to non-Christians than the old. Primitive ideas of God were discovered to correspond to Thomistic definitions, vestiges of a primitive revelation were everywhere found; 'primitive' peoples were apparently monotheistic and fully aware of the implications of the decalogue. This was well-meaning distortion, rather than outright rejection, but it remained at the level of ideas only. It made little difference in practice to the average missionary's day-to-day dealings with non-Christians.

In general, the average missionary before the Second Vatican Council was actively hostile to the practices of non-Christians. Where non-Christian religion was highly organized and institutionalized it was more difficult to give concrete expression to one's intolerance, but given a fragmented cultural situation with many competing ethnic groups and with the backing of the colonial power, it was easy enough to desecrate holy places, break up pagan gatherings, destroy shrines and so on. How many missions began with a missionary violating a pagan sacred place? In a certain mission church in Tanzania today the visitor is shown a large wooden baptismal font that was carved from the spirit tree cut down in anger by the first parish priest. Professor Tanner writing of Christianity in Sukumaland (Tanzania) remarks that the Sukuma people were convinced of one thing after the teaching of the missionaries, that 'to be a good Christian it was necessary to be a bad Sukuma'. The same could have been said of any number of missions, and this negative definition of Christianity, that entails the condemnation and rejection of everything in the pagan past, has been dinned into the heads of two or more generations of Christians.

If the early missionaries had not been spiritual giants they would not have got away with what they did, but they were holy men, of immense courage and personality. Their goodness was transparent, and their intolerance, though completely baffling to non-Christians, was nevertheless forgiven. People speak of them to day with love and admiration, and are proud of them even though they disagree with some of the things they did.

The implications of the pre-Vatican II attitude were that the Church was detached from the world and from human cultures. It was a self-servicing Church, serving its own ends, and not obviously relevant to ordinary human problems at all. It had, of course, to exist in some cultural form, and this form was decidedly western or European. Unthinkingly, the Church was engaged in the iconoclastic enterprise of destroying human cultures and of introducing alienation and division. This is not to say that missionaries were alone responsible for the break-up of the old order, or that this old order was a paradise on earth. Far from it. The non-Christian societies into which the missionaries came were not harmonious, idyllic communities, timeless and without change. Human societies are always changing. They have their own internal history and rhythm of evolution. External agents, such as foreign missionaries, may speed up this change, or introduce more far-reaching change, but they are still part of the larger process. Moreover, there were tensions and disharmonies in traditional societies which may have rendered their members less happy than after the missionaries came. The fact remains, however, that the missionary had a largely negative and destructive approach to non-Christian cultures, however much he may have esteemed and loved non-Christians as human beings. It was imperfectly understood that human beings are not cultural Robinson Crusoes, that they have a cultural personality and that this has to be taken into account when preaching Christ to them. There are no Christian values which are not human values, and human values that belong to a particular human culture. Christianity is not in itself a culture, but it supposes a cultural dress which must be either western or non-western. The negative aspects of missionary thinking before Vatican II were not without fruit. It was this experience that gave birth to a more developed theology of salvation and a more developed theology of cultures.

CHAPTER 3

Old Testament Revelation and the Church's Mission

We are now engaged in a renewal of our thinking about the Church's mission, that is to say, we are trying to discover God's purposes for us at this time and in the world in which we live. In this renewal the first source to which we must turn for help is the revealed Word of God. The Word of God is a person, Christ, and he is revealed to us in our life-situations, in our communities and social relationships, through faith illumined by the inspired Scriptures. The Old Testament slowly unfolds God's plan, which is fully revealed in Christ. It can, of course, only be understood in the light of Christ's life and message, but it was built up according to processes which are valid equally for the New Testament and for the continuing 'Revelation' of Christ in our own time, namely an understanding of the present through a faith illumined by a knowledge of past events. In this chapter we shall examine some themes from the Old Testament; in the next chapter we shall concentrate on the person of Christ himself. As far as possible we shall try to understand what the Bible has to tell us who live in the second half of the twentieth century.

The first important fact which the Old Testament tells us is that mankind is one – one in its origin, one in its destiny. Unity of origin is the clear lesson of Genesis. God is the origin of man and man is made to his 'image and likeness'. God stands at the apex of a pyramid which fans out over the centuries, through the first human couple, Adam 'man', and Eve 'mother of all those who live'. The first parents were commanded to increase and multiply, to fill the earth and to conquer it. In Chapter 10 of Genesis all the people of the earth were put into a single genealogical table, including even the Canaanites and the Egyptians and other enemies of Israel. All were accounted men and descendants of Noah, although their hostility was derived etiologically from the disrespect shown by Ham to his father.

Throughout the Old Testament great emphasis is placed upon the identity and integrity of God's people. The Israelites became God's people through the covenant they made with him, a covenant which was renewed on many solemn occasions in Israel's history, and, indeed, renewed liturgically every year in the temple. However, this covenant did not really set Israel above other people, or even wholly apart from other peoples. Israel was not to dominate others with a human or material power:

> For you are a people consecrated to Yahweh your God; it is you that Yahweh has chosen to be his very own people out of all the peoples on the earth. If Yahweh set his heart on you and chose you, it was not because you outnumbered other peoples, you were the least of all peoples (Deut 7.6-7).

Yet, if need arose, and if it was God's purpose, Israel could conquer and devour nations stronger than herself. In her dealings with other peoples Israel was not to make any covenant with them, or serve their gods. Moreover, there was to be no intermarriage:

> You must not marry with them: you must not give a daughter of yours to a son of theirs, nor take a daughter of theirs for a son of yours... (Deut 7.3).

Nevertheless, the rule was broken time and again, and paradoxically it was from such irregular unions with the pagans that the kingly line and the ancestry of the Messiah himself was traced, through Tamar the Canaanite, Rahab the harlot and Ruth the Moabite.

Ruth, who gave the classic example of filial piety in wishing to provide a legal descendant for her father-in-law, was one of the 'holy pagans' found repeatedly in the pages of the Old Testament. Abraham himself was called from the pagan culture of Ur of the Chaldees to begin the whole spiritual Odyssey of Israel. Melchizedek, King of Salem, was a priest of the Most High, the pagan priest who received tithes from Abraham, and who became, in Jewish traditions, the figure of the Messiah himself. Cyrus, king of Persia, is actually called 'the anointed of Yahweh' in the prophecy of Isaiah, being likened to the kings of Israel. These are reminders that Israel was only set apart from the nations in order, ultimately, to be integrated with them. God did not confine his saving activity to the bounds of Israel alone.

In the early days of her history, Israel had to struggle to defend her patrimony, to realize her religious ideal and to live among the pagan nations without being corrupted by them. Then came the Babylonian Captivity and the dispersal of the Jews all over the ancient world. This diaspora demanded an even greater level of detachment and purification. The religious ideal was spiritualized and interiorized. When they came out of Babylon where they had dwelt for so long, the Israelites were bidden by Isaiah to 'touch nothing unclean' as they came out of her. Their ideals there were just as uncompromising, even though they were dispersed among the nations. After the Exile they realized more clearly than before that Israel's destiny was not that of a politically powerful or materially wealthy nation which could rival other nations. They also realized that they had a mission to the whole world, that their religion was a universal one.

This universalism found expression in the psalms, in the book of Jonah and in the prophecies of Isaiah, Hosea, Amos, Micah and Malachi. A time would come when all the nations would be incorporated into Israel under the rule of the Messianic King. At times this state of affairs was represented as being the result of physical conquest: 'He brings the people under our dominion' (Ps 47.3); 'God, in fury bring the nations down!' (Ps 56.7). But, gradually, more emphasis was placed upon a peaceful solution. The great return of all the nations to Yahweh will follow upon the witness of Israel's sufferings. The nations will stream to Mount Zion, to worship in the temple. Jerusalem is the home of all the nations and their return will be a final homecoming. 'The whole earth, from end to end, will remember and come back to Yahweh' (Ps 22.27). All nations will praise the name of Yahweh, and there will be peace forever. Salvation will be achieved through incorporation into Israel:

> Let no foreigner who has attached himself to Yahweh say: 'Yahweh will surely exclude me from his people.' For Yahweh says this: ...'Foreigners who have attached themselves to Yahweh to serve him and to love his name and be his servants – all who observe the sabbath, not profaning it, and who cling to my covenant – these I will bring to my holy mountain. I will make them joyful in my house of prayer. Their holocausts and their sacrifices will be accepted on my altar, for my house will be called a house of prayer for all the peoples.' (Is 56.3-7).

This was to be the era of true worship, the pure offerings that Malachi spoke of, as being made from east to west, among the peoples. However, in spite of the incorporation envisaged by these texts, the nations, and particularly Israel herself, appear to retain their identities. The universalist religion of Israel is not separate from her national identity, and it is not yet seen just how a religion identified with one nation can be suited to all nations. It is against the background of this basic dilemma that the life and ministry of Jesus Christ has to be understood. He was the Messianic King whose coming was foretold and who was to resolve the dilemma, by changing the movement of universal salvation from a centripetal force concentrated upon the Old Israel into a centrifugal force emanating from the New Israel.

Christ was to show us that his message was not linked essentially with any one nation or culture, and that his teaching was a wholly new departure for mankind. We can trace a clear line of evolution in Old Testament Revelation leading to the final *impasse* from which Christ rescued us. In spite of this we are continually tempted to return to that *impasse* and to take an Old Testament view of universal salvation. It is essentially an Old Testament view of mission, to associate Christianity with a particular cultural tradition, to set the Church apart from the nations as an object of divine favouritism and to see nothing but evil in the religious traditions of non-Christians.

So far we have been considering the progressive revelation of universal salvation in the Old Testament from a positive angle, and it has led to an unresolved dilemma. Let us now look at Old Testament teaching from the negative angle. As we have seen, the Old Testament teaches mankind's original unity. It also teaches the progressive disruption of this unity – the introduction of more and more division and disharmony through sin. The origin of mankind's unity is

God himself, but by turning his back on God man destroys this unity. The revolt of man against God is followed by the revolt of man against man. The classic instance of this is the story of the murder of Abel by his brother Cain. The scattering of the peoples over the face of the earth is also explained by the authors of Genesis as a punishment for sin. The 'priestly' narrative takes, as we have seen, a positive view. All the nations are placed on a single genealogy and their dispersal is attributed to Yahweh's blessing of Noah, a repetition of the first blessing to Adam and Eve: 'Be fruitful, multiply and fill the earth.' The 'Yahwistic' narrative takes a negative view. The dispersal of the nations is due to the sin of pride: 'Come they said let us build ourselves a town and a tower with its top reaching heaven. Let us make a name for ourselves, so that we may not be scattered about the whole earth' (Gen 11.4). Yahweh came down to see what they were doing: 'This is but the start of their undertakings! There will be nothing too hard for them to do. Come let us go down and confuse their language on the spot so that they can no longer understand one another.' (Gen 11.7-8). Work stopped on the building of the tower because men could no longer understand one another. There was nothing to do but scatter over the face of the earth.

The story of the tower of Babel is the story of a breakdown in human communication. Men no longer understood one another. In the mind of the 'Yahwistic' narrator this accounted for the diversity of nations, cultures and languages. Cultural diversity was due to the failure to understand one another, and this failure was a consequence of sin. Diversity in this way of thinking is sinful. It is a 'scattering', a 'confusion', the very reverse of creation. The most frequent image of diversity in the Jewish culture was dust. Dust signified the indeterminate, the sinful. It was also a sign of sorrow and confusion. Dust was placed on the head as a sign of repentance for sin, or of mourning for a calamity. But it was of 'dust from the soil' that Adam was fashioned by God, because creation was a positive act. When man sinned he opted for that primeval dust, that negation of his being. This is certainly one legitimate way of looking at cultural diversity, to see the different cultural traditions of mankind as so many barriers to understanding and even communication. The globetrotter who takes a superficial look at the different cultures of the twentieth-century world, united, as they are, in subservience to a universal technology originating from the west, may jump to the conclusion that the world is just a 'big village', but how far from the truth he is! As if men wore their cultural personalities on their sleeves! The truth is that men are very deeply divided from one another, both as individuals and as collectivities, and these divisions become even more apparent in the so-called 'technopolis'.

However, the ancient Hebrews drew a distinction between diversity and multiplicity. Multiplicity belongs to the notion of creation, diversity to destruction. The Creator commanded Adam and Noah to 'be fruitful and multiply', to fill and conquer the earth. In obedience to this command, man has not only multiplied his own species, but he has multiplied his resources, his efficiency, his range of actions. He has multiplied his own possibilities. He has truly filled and conquered the earth – and he has not stopped short at the earth! Multiplicity is a blessing, diversity a curse. Multiplicity supposes harmony and co-operation between the multiple elements, diversity supposes sin, enmity, ill-will, pride.

We cannot, therefore, accept the Yahwistic etiology, if it means that the distinctive character of the different human cultures is essentially due to enmity and pride. The Yahwistic writer is concentrating on one aspect of culture – its abuse. The fact that there are many different cultures is also an opportunity for harmony and co-operation. Love supposes a relationship between two or more persons or collectivities. Once again the Old Testament cannot satisfy us completely; it is awaiting fulfilment in Jesus Christ. The story of the tower of Babel can only be understood in the light of what happened at Pentecost when unity was restored to mankind by the Pentecostal gift of tongues. At Pentecost the Spirit of love was given to men, to break down the barriers that separated Jew from Greek and nation from nation. All present heard the 'marvels of God'. The confusion and misunderstanding of the tower of Babel were removed and communication was again restored, but cultural uniformity was not. Cultural pluralism remained as before. Indeed, the unity of purpose effected by the Holy Spirit was manifested through a multiplicity of tongues. The flame separated into many tongues of fire which rested on the head of each, and this visible manifestation was associated with the many tongues spoken by the apostles. 'They were all filled with the Holy Spirit and began to speak foreign languages as the Spirit gave them the gift of speech' (Acts 2.4). The universal language of love spoken now by the apostles is common to all cultures, all nations, all tongues, and it demands such pluralism, such variety. Glossolaly (the speaking of incomprehensible sounds) was not an essential concomitant of the giving of the Holy Spirit. Its value was as a sign of the nature of this gift, and a sign, as St Paul told the Corinthians, for the pagans and unbelievers (1 Cor 14.22). Henceforward, the followers of Christ did not need glossolaly, but they would act, not on the principle of cultural uniformity which sought to incorporate all nations into a single culture, nor yet on the assumption of the Babel story that communication between cultures was impossible, but on the belief that the new creation, like the old, demanded multiplicity – even an expanding multiplicity, unified, not by tongue, but by the Spirit of Love.

CHAPTER 4

The Risen Life of Christ, Foundation of Our Mission

A Muslim friend of mine once told me: 'The trouble with you Christians is that you have a theology of anxiety.' He was referring to the present climate of self-criticism among western Christians who appear to be increasingly unsure of themselves. It is perfectly true, there is anxiety and insecurity. Christians are asking themselves: 'What right have I to teach my religion to peoples in other parts of the world, people who may be perfectly happy already with their own non-Christian religions? What right have I to change another man and to teach him needs of which he was formerly unaware?' Some are even so cynical as to tell you that the first thing missionaries teach people is about mortal sin – in order to create a need for the sacrament of penance and the other sacraments! 'What these people consciously need is food, medicine, education, human rights,' they say. 'Missionaries should stay at home and let Africans and Asians find out about the Gospel for themselves – if they want to.'

There are many reasons for this uncertainty and self-criticism; the exploding of the myth of western racial, moral and cultural superiority, the growth of secularism and the consequent failure to relate unconscious religious needs to conscious material ones and so on. One important reason is surely the inadequacy of the preconciliar theology of mission, perhaps even a radical misunderstanding of the nature of the Christian life itself? People just did not see what missionary activity had to do with their lives as Christians. As we have seen, they thought of the missions as marginal areas in an abnormal situation, needing special solutions and a special – if not a specialist – corps of workers. The missions were an extra, resulting from a mandate. Perhaps, even that mandate was an afterthought. First came the commands of Christ concerning Christian discipleship; then came the final order: 'Go, teach all nations whatsoever I have commanded you.'

In reality it is the nature of Christ and his risen life which makes the Church missionary. The mandate is simply one way of expressing this. The Christian is configured to Christ, and the Church, the People of God to which the Christian belongs, is the prolongation of Christ's work. It follows that the Christian and the Church to which he belongs will not be essentially missionary unless Christ himself is essentially missionary. The mission derives not from a mere word, but from the Word that is life, and that Word also is 'Go'.

Christians today are indulging in self-criticism about the propriety of missionary work, but they are also examining their consciences about the propriety of enjoying too much of the world's material wealth while others starve, the problem of the haves and the have-nots. Is the western Christian justified in keeping his wealth for himself? Most westerners with a Christian conscience would answer 'No.' It comes as rather a shock to find that this was exactly St Paul's attitude to the Gospel. St Paul actually felt that he owed the Gospel to the pagans, that he had no right to keep it from them. Preaching was a duty that he neglected at the risk of punishment, although it was the love of Christ, rather than the fear of punishment, which drove him on to proclaim the Good News. Peter and John felt the same way. People had a right to know what the apostles had experienced. 'We cannot promise', they told the Sanhedrin, 'to stop proclaiming what we have seen and heard' (Acts 4.20). There was nothing to be embarrassed about: 'For I am not ashamed of the Good News: it is the power of God saving all who have faith' (Rom 1.16).

However, the mission is not simply a question of haves and have-nots, of the lucky being kind to the unlucky. All giving has to be two-sided, as the western world is discovering in its clumsy attempts at aiding the poorer nations, and this means that the bigot is as unacceptable as lady bountiful. No one can be a missionary who has a 'holier than thou' attitude. No one can give who is not also ready to give himself, as St Paul reminded the Thessalonians: 'We were eager to hand over to you not only the Good News but our whole lives as well' (I Thess 2.8). More than this, the Good News about Christ is not something that can be taught. Christ is experienced. The Gospel is a living reality, not a book, and it is understood less by reading books and listening to sermons and exhortations than by communion among and between people. The Gospel is a way of life – a sharing, a mutual fulfilment, a *koinonia*. Because of this, no one who accepts it can keep it to himself. Living the Gospel means accepting the mission and accepting to be missionary. To refuse to share it is to betray the Gospel.

At the end of the last chapter we saw how Old Testament Israel was left with the unsolved problem of how to reconcile its loyalty to a national culture with a universal vocation. Christ solved that problem by refusing to identify religion with any particular culture. This meant, not only that cultural differences were no longer barriers to human communication at the deepest levels, but that being a Christian would be an endless voyage of discovery, an endless enrichment. The missionary-Christian would be continually recognizing new faces of Christ. He would be receiving as much as, and more than, he gave. Christ effected this solution through his resurrection. Jesus adopted our humanity in order to transform us, but our humanity is incapable of communicating life outside itself. This was the physical life of the old Adam, the 'flesh' which includes its animating principle, the living human soul. 'The flesh', says St John, 'has nothing to offer, it is the spirit that gives life' (Jn 6.64). Through his death and resurrection Christ was changed from a living soul into a life-giving spirit. 'The first man Adam, as scripture says, became a living soul; but the last Adam has become a life-giving spirit' (1 Cor 15.44). Christ was raised to life by the Spirit of God. He was anointed with the Spirit, the Power of God. His being was so penetrated and saturated by the Spirit that he could not merely be described as 'spiritual'. He 'is' Spirit. As St Paul says, speaking of our reflecting the glory of Jesus: 'All grow brighter and brighter as we are turned into the image that we reflect; this is the work of the Lord who is Spirit.' (2 Cor

3.18). The risen Christ did not lose his personality, nor was the person of the Son confused in any way with the person of the Holy Spirit, but he has been filled with the living power of the Holy Spirit to such an extent that his flesh has been transformed and he has become, in his manhood, the full and final life-giving reality of God. This reality overflows the limitations of his historic manhood, and now gives life to the world. Christ becomes many while remaining one, and the many become one in him, while remaining themselves.

The risen life of Christ, in which all Christians share, is not therefore, a treasure for private enjoyment, it is a dispersal, a scattering, of self. It is not a centripetal force, spiralling inwards to an individual person, or an individual culture, but a centrifugal force spiralling outwards to embrace more and more individual persons and cultures. The risen life is the ability to transcend one's own limitations and to communicate with – even to exist for – others. A man cannot conclude from the fact that he is a convinced Christian that he ought to work for the missions, but rather that his Christian convictions are wanting if he is not actively interested in the Church's mission. If he is not interested in other people, in other cultures, in bringing the Good News to them, and if he is not doing something about it, can he really say that he shares in the risen life of Christ? The risen Christ is perceived through the Spirit in interpersonal, social and cultural relationships. Every Christian has the clear duty to seek and find him, in the measure in which knowledge and opportunity is given him. This is what is meant by saying that the Church or the Christian is essentially missionary. The primary reason for the existence of the Church, the primary reason for the existence of the Christian, the experiencing of the risen Christ, is realized through missionary activity.

The Good News we bring is that God is in Christ, God breaking through the limitations of an earthly life, in the power of the resurrection, and reconciling or unifying humanity. 'It is all God's work. It was God who reconciled us to himself through Christ and gave us the work of handing on this reconciliation. In other words, God in Christ was reconciling the world to himself, not holding men's faults against them, and he has entrusted to us the news that they are reconciled' (2 Cor 5.18-19). Christ's work, in other words, and the work of the Church which prolongs it, is a work of unification, of making the nations into a single

People of God. It is a work which breaks down barriers between individuals and groups, all the discriminatory barriers which divide races, religions, classes, nationalities and even the sexes. This is why the Church must stand out against racial discrimination, against religious intolerance, against class-consciousness, tribalism, exaggerated nationalism and the inferior status of women. Speaking of Jew and Gentile, St Paul declared: 'He is the peace between us, and has made the two into one and broken down the barrier which used to keep them apart, actually destroying in his own person the hostility caused by the rules and decrees of the Law. This was to create one single New Man in himself out of the two of them, and by restoring peace through the cross, to unite them both in a single body and reconcile them with God' (Eph 2. 15-6). 'There are no more distinctions between Jew and Greek, slave and free, male and female, but all of you are one in Christ Jesus' (Gal 3.28).

'Making the many one' is a contradiction in terms for everyone except the Christian who has really understood Christ. Unification does not mean forcing uniformity, reducing everything to a single blueprint or common denominator. Unification is not 'a conquest of the nations' for Christ, a spiritual form of imperialism. It means spreading the mentality of co-operation, mutual understanding, optimism, justice and the desire for peace. It means the union of everyone in the desire for the good of each other, in ultimate respect for each other. In short, it means love, and the Spirit with which the risen Christ was anointed is the Spirit of Love. It is only selfless love that respects the multiplicity of individuals and cultures; it is only within such multiplicity and pluriformity that genuine love can operate and find scope. Configuration to Christ makes the Christian capable of this love, but this love is not a purely intellectual thing. It has to be practised. The Christian can only find Christ, can only participate in his risen life, by serving and spending himself for others. In missionary activity he discovers Christ. It is the love of Christ which gathers the many into one, and it is the love of Christ which makes the whole experiment worthwhile. In Christ alone is it possible to plumb the depths of human personality and to appreciate the riches of human culture. The knowledge of Christ draws us deeper and further in this search than any mere human knowledge. Consequently, the love of Christ is capable of the strictest and most profound reconciliation between men. There is no unity so profound as unity in the love of Christ.

An important conclusion of what has just been said is that, if the Christian life is properly understood, the Church should be self-propagating. There should be no dearth of vocations, no lack of missionaries, no stagnation or isolation. This is not the same thing as saying that there ought to be a constant, absolute, numerical increase of baptized Christians, priests or missionaries, and we shall discuss in a later chapter how, in practice, the Church realizes the universality of her mission. What is meant here is that if the nature of the Christian life is properly understood, there should be no 'missionary eras' of the Church. No Vicar of Christ should be called 'the Pope of the missions' (as if some popes were more missionary than others). Nobody should look upon the missions as an exceptional or a temporary situation, because the whole Church is always and everywhere missionary. If the Church is not constantly discovering Christ in new cultures and fresh situations, then she is failing in her vocation. She is even misunderstanding the meaning of the love of Christ, because the love of Christ is by definition an active love, a love which attracts and makes new Christians. A missionary Church means therefore a self-propagating Church.

The mission of the Church has been described here as the experience of the risen Christ in a loving exchange between men – an essay in human communications that is successful because it is also a divine experiment. It follows that such a mission has two dimensions. The first dimension is the horizontal one – expansion. This does not mean necessarily numerical expansion, but it does mean that the Church must be continually entering areas where Christ is not explicitly acknowledged, and re-entering areas where, due to radical changes, the knowledge of Christ has been forgotten. We are not talking here of a strictly spatio-temporal expansion, therefore, but of a continual journey through the multiple, changing circumstances of man. It is a continual identification with, and adaptation to, successive personal, social and cultural experiences. Such experiences have extension, of course, in space and time, but the emphasis is on the variety, the multiplicity of these experiences. To use the Pauline metaphor, all these experiences have to be brought to the Church, so that it eventually becomes 'the perfect Man, fully mature with the fulness of Christ himself' (Eph 4.13). There is thus a sense in which even Christ, albeit eternally, is brought to completion, filling mankind with his fulness. '...There is no room for distinction between Greek and Jew, between the circumcised or the uncircumcised, or between barbarian and Scythian, slave and free man. There is only Christ: he is everything and he is in everything' (Col 3.10-11). 'And when everything is subjected to him, then the Son will be subject in his turn to the One who subjected all things to him, so that God may be all in all' (1 Cor 15.28).

The second dimension is one of penetration. The knowledge of Christ enables man to penetrate the different facets and levels of human life more deeply. It is a greater interiorization of man's experience. Man has received the command, not merely to increase and multiply, personally and culturally, but also to fill the earth and subdue it. His task is to humanize his world, to probe and to understand his environment from every angle, to develop and use all his talents and all that nature offers. All created things, nature and technology, are restored in Christ. It is part of the Church's mission to use all of this to foster the communion of mankind in the love of Christ.

The missionary Christian must therefore realize both dimensions of his vocation, otherwise he stunts the risen life in him, but the degree to which, in practice, he realizes either depends on his response to the talents and opportunities which God gives him.

CHAPTER 5

The Theology of Development

The story of the Tower of Babel has already figured in these pages as the symbol of human diversity and of the breakdown in human communication. It is also an eloquent object lesson about the consequences of a merely technical development.

> They said to one another, 'Come let us make bricks and bake them in the fire!' – For stone they used bricks, and for mortar they used bitumen. – 'Come', they said, 'let us build ourselves a town and a tower with its top reaching heaven. Let us make a name for ourselves, so that we may not be scattered about the whole earth.' (Gen 11.3-4).

The Jewish writer saw Babylon as the product of an advance in building techniques. It was no longer necessary to dress stone and mix mortar. With baked bricks and bitumen pitch one could build a skyscraping ziggurat. The sin of the Babylonians was not so much that they wanted to build a skyscraper, as that they wanted to 'make a name for themselves' by so doing. They gloried in a technical ability which served no other purpose than their pride. The tower was a prestige project which had nothing to do with the progress or welfare of the human community. On the contrary, like the pyramids, it was probably built by slave labour. God himself acknowledged that there were no limits to what man could do, but there was nothing wrong in this. Had he not told Adam to 'fill the earth and conquer it', and Noah to 'teem over the earth and be lord of it'? Now he complained: 'There will be nothing too hard for them to do!', not because he was rescinding his orders but because the Babylonians were reverting to the sin of empty pride evinced both by Adam and by those who perished in the flood. The tower of Babel could have been finished. It remained unfinished because it had no purpose or meaning. It was a folly.

The most important question that has to be asked about socio-economic development is: 'What is it all for?' Material development is not, and cannot be, an end in itself. The newly independent nations of Africa and Asia are concentrating all their forces on developing their countries, creating wealth for their people, and raising their standards of living. There is also heavy spending on education and medical services. Education, in particular, is being harnessed to manpower production, to turning out the necessary leaders and technicians. But this process is a means to an end – Man himself and his destiny. Development creates wealth, but wealth is no guarantee of human happiness. Development creates leisure but does not necessarily help a man to spend it enjoyably and profitably. Development can lengthen a man's life, but it need not make that life worth living. Education can turn a man into an efficient tool of development instead of educating him to be first of all a man. The important thing is that the process of development be a reasonable and a human process, aimed at creating a happy, human community, a community in which men are free to be themselves and to live the fullest possible human lives. This, in turn, requires that there be an ideology, or a system of values to give purpose and meaning to the process of socio-economic development.

The so-called humanist complains of the conflict between religious ideologies as an obstacle to development. Although he may appreciate that these ideologies are a driving force for development, his argument is that their disadvantages outweigh their advantages. The old-fashioned humanist used to proclaim a 'value-less development', but even he, sooner or later, would be trapped into speaking about 'happiness' or 'the common good' and would have to admit that he was now in the realm of values and priorities. In fact, there are any number of opinions about what 'happiness' or 'the common good' consist in, and if one is to find a workable ideology one must have the freedom to argue, to disagree and to make a choice between alternatives. It is impossible to operate a technology without values. As soon as atomic power was discovered, or as soon as human organic transplants became possible, a debate followed on how to use these discoveries and advances in technology. The techniques themselves could not provide the answer. The answer had to come from man himself and man's own value-systems. The only alternative is to abandon development altogether, as the Babylonians abandoned their unfinished tower.

I do not wish, in any way, to belittle the problems created by a conflict between competing ideologies and competing interest groups in a developing country. The government of such a country has to see that the differences do not become an obstacle to development. It can do this successfully in one of two ways. It can either make a religious ideology its own and therefore refuse to tolerate other religious ideologies, or it can create a political ideology which is in harmony with the essential tenets of the religions represented in the country, in which case it tacitly allows these religions to regard themselves as offering a development of that ideology. The government in question can either disregard these religious addenda or it can welcome their existence. Quite a number of African Socialist ideologies, for example, recognize the value of religious convictions. African Socialism has been described as 'non-atheist', and one African president has gone so far as to say that the African Socialist must be a believer, because it is only the believer who asks big questions. Big questions have to be asked if man is to make any progress. The African political ideologies lay considerable stress on man himself, and especially on man-in-community. For African leaders co-operative living is an ideal in itself, and at least two of them have defined the essential energy of the movement as 'love'. Such ideas are completely in harmony with Christianity, the task of which it is to build communities which breathe the Spirit of Love.

The differences that exist between one religious ideology and another can be viewed in a way analogous to cultural differences. Negatively, they generate 'polemic'; positively, they inspire 'dialogue'. They are examples of mankind's essential pluralism. To say that there should be only one ideology or value-system would mean that one believed that everything had been said about humanity that could be said. True religion, as we hope to show, does not believe that the last word has been said; for the discovery of purpose and meaning is no less a progressive movement than technical development. The religious believer does not set any limits to the humanizing process; he is always trying to be more human. The Christian, however, although he recognizes the diversity of religions *de facto,* has an ultimate faith in the unification of mankind, a unification that can only be achieved in Christ. As we have already seen, this unification does not destroy mankind's essential pluralism, but it marks a new beginning in the limitless development of man. The Christian has no special knowledge about when this unification will take place – whether, for example, it will be in history or outside of time altogether; but it is a glimpse of the unseen that lures him on. Ecumenism, therefore, is not a luxury; it is part of the process by which the world's religions will ultimately converge, even if this convergence is still impossibly obscure. The humanist is right to be impatient of religious polemic, and he is justifiably exasperated at the way non-essential religious differences are magnified. Ecumenism has to get down to the essentials and remain there, if it is to achieve anything at all.

Nevertheless, the final and most serious accusation of the humanist has yet to be considered. It is the accusation which echoes the charge of Marx and Engels that religion is essentially a form of alienation, that it directs man away from his world, from his own human problems to a world of make-believe, to 'pie in the sky'. It is the accusation that religion is an opium, a form of escapism, that absorbs human and material resources in a fruitless activity with never any tangible results to show for it. Seen thus, religion is the enemy of socio-economic development – a major cause of wastage, a useless luxury in material terms.

The unfairness of this accusation is that it attacks a monstrous caricature of religion to which certainly no Christian could subscribe. It is an attack on a perversion of religion which, whether or not it has been historically verified at any time, cannot be taken seriously as an ideal. The God whom the Christian worhips is not an alienation, nor does he direct man's attention away from humanity. On the contrary, he continually brings him back to the service of humanity and condemns the escapist interpretation of religion. There are instances of this on almost every page of scripture.

Adam and Noah were instructed, as we have seen, to multiply and to conquer the earth, the promises made to Abraham, Isaac and Jacob were all about an expanding nation that would enjoy prosperity, and victory; the promise to Moses and Aaron concerned a land flowing with milk and honey, and the quails and manna with which the Israelites were fed in the desert was a sign of this future, material abundance. Alone among the peoples of the Near East the Israelites were forbidden by their religion to make images of their God as a focus for worship. God dwelt among his people and if sacrifices and oblations were commanded, they were markedly expiatory in character, being so many expressions of the attempt to be 'an acceptable people' and to make amends for anti-social acts. Even the very commandments of God were predominantly about human relations and fidelity to them brought prosperity.

> I have heard this people's words. All they have spoken is well said. If only their heart were always so, set on the fear of me and the keeping of my commandments, so that they and their children might prosper for ever! (Deut 5.29).

Time and again, through the prophets, the attention of the Israelites was diverted away from temple worship and ceremonial prescriptions towards the task of building a truly human community.

> Yahweh Sabaoth, the God of Israel, says this: Amend your behaviour and your actions and I will stay with you. Put no trust in delusive words like these. This is the sanctuary of Yahweh, the sanctuary of Yahweh, the sanctuary of Yahweh! But if you do amend your behaviour and your actions, if you treat each other fairly, if you do not exploit the stranger, the orphan and the widow (if you do not shed innocent blood in this place), and if you do not follow alien gods to your own ruin, then here in this place I will stay with you, in the land that long ago I gave to your fathers for ever. Yet here you are, trusting in delusive words

to no purpose (Jer 7.3-8).

No one was more scathing than the prophet Amos:

> I hate and despise your feasts, I take no pleasure in your solemn festivals. When you offer me holocausts... I reject your oblations, and refuse to look at your sacrifices of fattened cattle, Let me have no more of the din of your chanting, no more of your strumming on harps. But let justice flow like water, and integrity like an unfailing stream' (Amos 5.21-24).

In the New Testament this view of religion is very much more pronounced. Jesus, himself, preferred the title 'Son of Man' to any other, and constantly used it. As Messiah, he was 'the firstborn of all creation', the head of the human race. His verbal contests with the Pharisees were a consistent onslaught on the view of religion condemned by the humanist. 'The sabbath was made for man, not man for the sabbath, so the Son of Man is master even of the sabbath' (Mk 2.27-28). The Gospel of Christ is a gospel of social action, of service, compassion and generosity – of deeds rather than words. Whenever Christ speaks of prayer and worship, it is almost always to expose the hypocrisy of those who put formal religion in the place of active community building. The follower of Christ has 'to pray always' through action, through his fidelity to the great Christian commandment of mutual love. St James certainly understood the spirit of Christianity when he gave his definition of religion: 'Pure, unspoilt religion, in the eyes of God our Father is this: coming to the help of orphans and widows when they need it and keeping oneself uncontaminated by the world.'(Jas 2.27).

In himself, Christ is the ultimate embodiment of the God of the Old Testament, the God who tells men to serve the human community. As we have seen, in the last chapter, it is in him that all men are reconciled, through the power of the Resurrection; and it is through him that the mentality of co-operation and mutual understanding is spread. Christian worship is centred on this Christ, the Son of Man; he is the new Temple which embraces the whole human race. The high point of Christian worship is the Eucharist and this Eucharist is very far from a form of alienation or escapism. The Eucharist is the foreshadowing – even the very first experience – of this ultimate reconciliation among men. At the celebration of the Eucharist Christians discover, and make explicit, their community in Christ and through

Christ their community with all men. Nothing could be more in harmony with mankind's development than this deliberate pointer towards the very goal of development.

Development can also be viewed theologically as a progressive liberation from evils both physical and spiritual. When this is so, physical and spiritual must not be separated, let alone opposed. The Christian might be tempted to over-emphasize the idea of spiritual liberation as a 'redressing of the balance' in a too materialistic view of development, and if he did this, he would lay himself open to the same, or similar, charges from the humanist as those with which we have just been dealing. Body and soul cannot in fact be separated; for the soul expresses itself bodily, and its destiny is some kind of a bodily destiny. We know very little about the 'spiritual' or 'risen' body and about its relationship to the new Earth, and this is perhaps the weakest part of the theology of development, but we know that Christ himself is the answer to these mysteries. Teilhard de Chardin has described the parousia very finely and very poetically: 'Like lightning, like a conflagration, like a flood, the attraction exerted by the Son of Man will lay hold of all the whirling elements in the universe so as to reunite them or subject them to his body' (*Le Milieu Divin,* London 1960, p. 151). The fact remains that, for no reason whatsoever, can the Church abdicate her responsibility for the body, and for the material development of mankind.

During his earthly life Christ spent a very great deal of his time healing the sick, feeding the hungry, visiting and consoling people, and educating and re-educating his hearers. The Church has always realized her mission through works of this kind. In very many of the so-called mission countries it was the Church that laid the foundations of the medical services and of the educational system; and it is the Church that continues to make the biggest contribution to them of any voluntary agency. The Church's relief services have also been an important factor in assisting the victims of famine, war and other disasters. It is the Church's mission to awaken the conscience of the industrialized nations so that the disproportion between the rich and the poor nations is corrected, and so that the excessive inequalities of economic power are removed by the application of principles of social justice and not perpetuated by the law of free competition, operating in a situation where one side has all the advantages. It is also the Church's mission to train and educate the young members of developing nations so that these countries can eventually stand on their own feet, – another way of bridging the gap between rich and poor nations.

In all of this the Church must be aware that she is dealing with human material, and that her ultimate aim is to build a happy human community where men are free to be themselves, and where love, justice and co-operation reign. She can only do this if she co-operates in the process of material development as the Body of Christ, if she is not ashamed of her mission to be the Sacrament of the World.

CHAPTER 6

The Church's Mission and Human Personality

Leopold Sedar Senghor, the African President of Senegal, writing about the relevance of belief in God for African Socialism, had this to say: 'If one places love of the Super-Person above human love, there will naturally be a powerful attraction to group individuals without constraint' (*On African Socialism,* London 1964, p. 147). Senghor's problem was how to have socialization without depersonalization – how to build a community without sacrificing the individual to the collectivity. If the collectivity is merely a technical organization it does not attract individuals, it must constrain them. Senghor suggests that there must be a human convergence, and a convergence towards the love of a Super-Person if there is to be a real community. That is why, he believes, the African Socialist should not only tolerate, but actively encourage, religious belief.

The Christian maintains that the fact of Jesus Christ is decisive for an understanding of the human person – even for the very nature of personalness. Jesus Christ is the definition of personalness. He is the Super-Person. It is very difficult to say just what being a person means. Being a person is an experience; it means being an 'I', and being an 'I' in relation to other 'I's. It means having an awareness of oneself in relation to others. An essential feature of being a person is the capacity to enter into personal relationships or relationships which refer to your peculiarly human potentialities and our very existence as human beings. It is through being treated as a person, and through experiencing personal relationships that one comes to some sort of an understanding of what a person is. Ultimately, a personal relationship is a relationship of love, a relationship in which one understands, respect and loves another for himself, and is in turn loved by the other for himself. It is a mutual interiorization, which is the foundation of human happiness, since happiness consists in understanding and being understood, in loving and being loved.

However, in saying that one loves another person for himself, one is not saying that one wants to possess him, or keep him as he is, still less to mould him into an image of oneself. That would merely be treating him as a thing to be used, rather than a person to be respected and loved. A personal relationship goes beyond the persons who enter into it. It is an adventure which opens on to something greater, something unknown to both parties. In short, it is love for the sake of love. If one wants to be a person and enjoy that indefinable experience we call a personal relationship, one must believe in love for its own sake. Without faith in the existence, the permanence and the worthwhileness of that love, there is no personalness and no possibility of really being ourselves. Christianity offers mankind the faith which makes it possible to be a person, concerned with persons. God, revealed in Jesus Christ, is love itself, love personified, Senghor's Super-Person.

As the gospels show him to us, there is no doubt that Jesus Christ was concerned with persons. He believed in personal service and contact. When sick people were brought to him, he laid his hands on each of them, as Luke tells us. His interest in the downtrodden and his compassion for the sick were constant signs of his personal concern. So also was his use of personal names. In all cultures the name is an extension of the person and when Jesus called Mary of Magdala by her name, she recognized him instantly. This fact is not unimportant because it shows that if Mary understood the Resurrection through a personal relationship with the risen Christ, we also are to encounter the risen Christ through personal relationships. Indeed, it is not merely through Christ's example that we appreciate his concern for persons, but it is chiefly through his death and through the manner in which his Resurrection operates that we experience it. 'A man can have no greater love than to lay down his life for his friends' (Jn 15.13). Christ is the 'first to be born from the dead' (Col 1.18); he has given his flesh 'for the life of the world' (Jn 6.51); and he is the one who 'fills the whole creation' (Eph 1.23). 'No one has ever seen God; but as long as we love one another God will live in us and his love will be complete in us' (1 Jn 4.12). Through the Resurrection the divine person who was also fully human made human personality explicit, because he supplied the direction and the impetus of personal development.

Christ has provided us with the point of convergence which is indispensable for an understanding of humanity and for the bringing into existence of human communities. 'God wanted all perfection to be found in him and all things to be reconciled through him and for him' (Col 1.19). In Christ, we know that man has a common goal and that this goal is not only the purpose of all human association but the very means of association, making the association worthwhile for itself. Although human life is essentially a life in common and human personality depends on this basic fact, we still have it within us to dehumanize and depersonalize ourselves, to opt out of the community and to act for selfish motives. Given this possibility, we need the attraction of the Super-Person to draw men freely together. Constraint depersonalizes man, because it reduces man to the impersonal and robs him of the freedom to develop as a person. Freedom is of the essence of personalness.

To go back to the tower of Babel once more, the tower was a folly because it did not contribute to the convergence or reconciliation of men. It was a source of rivalry and division. Merely technical development cannot contribute to personalness, and only personalness can give meaning to materiality. Man is a part of the material universe, and in so far as he is material, he is determined by it. Science and technology advance by neutral, impersonal and deterministic methods, but such methods cannot be applied uncritically to man himself without robbing him of his freedom and personality. Man cannot be reduced to a set of statistics, or to a list of component physical substances. One of the stumbling-blocks in the social sciences has been precisely the tendency to regard the study of man as a 'science' in the physical science sense, rather than as a 'humanity'. Every day we meet an over-optimistic scientism which makes exaggerated claims to be a panacea for all mankind's ills, but science on its own is neither helpful nor harmful. Everything depends on the good and bad use that men make of its achievements and discoveries, and the criterion of what is good and bad is what helps or hinders the development of personalness. It follows also that the very development of science and technology depends on the survival of personalness, otherwise science will destroy itself, or at the very least, cease to have any relevance. It is personalness, therefore, that sets the material universe free for science to study, and it is personalness that ensures scientific and technological development.

Belief in Jesus Christ is the guarantee of the survival of personalness. All persons, all things are summed up in him:

> He is the image of the unseen God and the firstborn of all creation, for in him were created all things in heaven and on earth: everything visible and everything invisible, Thrones, Dominations. Sovreignties, Powers – all things were created through him and for him. Before anything was created, he existed, and he holds all things in unity (Col 1.15-17).

As David Jenkins has very finely written:

> Jesus Christ shows that a truly human person, a real man, is an individual who is wholly and consistently open to all possibilities of materiality and history as they impinge upon him, to all the demands and possibilities of other persons as he encounters them, and to the reality of God which is both involved in materiality, historicity and other persons and also exists independently and transcendentally. Such a real man has never yet existed save in the defining case of Jesus Christ, but this is the reality of which all men to some extent partake, for which all men are destined and in which all men will find complete fulfilment of their existence. It is human 'nature', all that is involved in being a man (*The Glory of Man,* London, 1967, pp. 91-92).

The preaching of the Super-Person, Jesus Christ, is altogether relevant for the human progress to which developing nations are committed, but we must beware of any hint of ethno-centricity in our personalist theology. More important still, we must not confuse personalness with its perversion, individualism. In the writings of missiologists as well as of secular theologians, one sometimes finds an altogether mythical picture of tribal society. Primitive society, according to them, is characterized by a kind of herd-instinct in which the individual is not free to innovate. Instead he is like a robot, subject to the unchanging control of immemorial custom. Absence of change is the *sine qua non* of this collective life; and historical personalities cannot make any impact on it whatever. The individual does not have to think for himself; society does his thinking for him, through its unconscious collective representations. The individual is 'merged' with the group, 'submerged' in the group, 'fused' or even 'confused' with the group, 'sunk' into the group. From this situation, we are told, it is the task of Christianity to set him free, by teaching him individual responsibility and independence of action.

Needless to say, such a 'tribal' society does not, nor did it ever, exist. Such an idea derives from the picture of society painted by early social philosophers, sociologists and anthropologists, as an organism in which each part was subordinated to the whole. Such writers spoke as if society were almost a concrete, tangible thing, with its own personality and purposes. It was an essentially static view of society as a harmonious, working whole, and the primitive world was, in this view, made up of a series of discrete entities, each society being isolated from the other. Arising from this caricature of society in general and of primitive society in particular, came the hypothesis of an individualist 'breakthrough'. Popular sociology (which is always a dated sociology) is fond of telling us that we are entering the era of the 'open city', the technocratic age, in which man has no need of society, and in which interpersonal relationships are networks centred upon the individual. When theologians identify themselves with this questionable sociology, they run the risk of picturing the Church's mission to the non-western world as one of preaching the gospel of individualism to peoples in the grip of an unthinking collectivism.

These are extreme positions, far removed from reality. On the one hand, society is not a thing. It is individuals who make up society, and society is something which exists in the minds of individuals. The social structure is not visible or tangible, still less has it a will of its own. Individuals in society are not a structure, but they have a structure. A structure is a way of looking at the relationships between individuals. Nevertheless, society and social structure are very real facts, even though they are of the logical order, and they are facts which exercise some sort of compulsion upon individuals, who are to a very great extent the products of their society. The mistake is to confuse personalness with individualism. Personalness stands between collectivism and individualism, between the individual and his society; it is the product of an interaction between the two.

The study of the so-called 'primitive' societies shows unmistakably that personalness existed in them, even if it was at a restricted level. There was a tension between the individual and the group. This is shown in the fact that, while production was largely individual, consumption through mandatory gift-exchange was communal. It is also shown in the initiation-rites by which tensions between the individual and society were worked out at moments when society made very special demands on individuals. It is shown in the opposition between structure and anti-structure in rituals and secret societies, through which people underwent a transforming experience that went to the root of each person's being and found in that root something profoundly communal and shared, rituals in which they rediscovered their personal freedom and their sentiment for humanity. Nothing could be further from the truth than the picture of a rigid, unchanging, social structure, isolated and uninfluenced from outside. Every structure has to be challenged, otherwise it has no frame of reference. It has to be challenged from within by an appeal to human freedom It has to be challenged from without by historical forces which stimulate change. The analysis of myths and rituals reveals that they refer to a process, a configuration of events and personalities that is ultimately a history. In Africa, at least, recent studies have shown how flexible traditional societies were, and how open to the movement of ideas. Gone is the vision of an unchanging, eternally stagnant society, without history and without progress.

Of course, one can legitimately complain that the wheels of pre-colonial African history ground slowly, and that the scope of personal interaction and fulfilment was restricted to small ethnic and family groupings. But a balanced personalness was there, without collectivist and individualist deviations, and this tradition of the 'individual in community' has become the ideal of a modern African socialism. President Julius Nyerere of Tanzania has written, for example:

> Our first step, therefore, must be to re-educate ourselves; to regain our former attitude of mind. In our traditional African society we were individuals within a community. We took care of the community, and the community took care of us. We neither needed nor wished to exploit our fellow men. (*Ujamaa*, Oxford, 1968, pp. 6-7).

However, an effort has now to be made to accelerate the

pace of human development, to overstep the limited horizons of clan, family, village and chiefdom while appealing to the same basic personal values. This does not mean abandoning the reality of the local community, but it does mean opening up the local community to broader outside influences and making possible co-operation on a wider scale through increased mobility of population and through the adoption of nation-wide loyalties and development aims.

In this context the Church has an obvious role to play. Whether she comes into a situation in which human beings are in process of being depersonalized through an exaggerated collectivism or an exaggerated individualism, or whether the situation, by itself, offers opportunities for personal development, the Church can still make a decisive contribution by pointing to Christ who is all at once the definition, the impetus and the goal of personal development.

CHAPTER 7

The Church's Mission and Human Cultures

Sir Edwin Tylor, a well-known nineteenth century ethnologist, once defined culture as: 'that complex whole which includes knowledge, belief, art, morals, law, custom and any other capabilities and habits acquired by man as a member of society' (*Primitive Culture,* London, 1891). This is a comprehensive or descriptive definition, but the operative words are 'acquired by man as a member of society.' The individual is taught by his society and receives his cultural identity through his society. It is culture that makes a man an Englishman rather than a Frenchman, a Muganda rather than a Kikuyu, a Japanese rather than a Chinaman. We have seen that it is the task of Christ to break down barriers between peoples and 'to make the nations one', that the new creation demands a cultural multiplicity which is summed up in Christ. We have to ask now how this is brought about in practice. We have seen that the person only finds fulfilment through the relationship with other persons. Is it also true that the culture acquires an understanding of itself through an exchange with other cultures? This is no mere academic question; it is a question which affects us very deeply since every man's personality is a cultural personality.

Writers and thinkers have not been lacking who proclaimed a unilinear evolution in which a single culture, the European or Western Culture, plays the decisive role. Christopher Dawson, Arnold Toynbee and Teilhard de Chardin are all writers who, in their various ways, give pride of place to western culture in the scheme of world development. The idea of a world culture or a technological culture is attractive to westerners and it seems to coincide with the reality of the political and economic domination of the rest of the world by the west. However much Africans and Asians may reject western values, westerners can console themselves that the West is making its impact just the same. It is a relentless, inevitable process.

The Church has never subscribed to so blunt and so complacent a view of cultural evolution, but up until the Second Vatican Council it was tacitly assumed that Roman Catholicism has to be some kind of a cultural monolith. This was the so-called 'Constantinian' picture of the Church. Missiologists usually employed horticultural metaphors when writing about this topic. In their conception, the Church had its own culture, which was in a continuous state of development. It was a Jewish culture on to which had been grafted in turn Hellenic, Latin, Germanic, Nordic and Saxon elements. Each graft became merged with the previously existing stock. Thus in mission lands the cultures of Africa and Asia were also to be similarly grafted and merged.

This theory did not, in fact, do justice to the real state of affairs. Christian culture as it developed was not an obvious hybrid and the grafted elements did not merge so much as become submerged in a single basic culture, the Graeco-Roman culture. The history of the Church in Europe has been the history of one pagan culture after another collapsing and being replaced by the already Christianized Graeco-Roman culture. In the Middle Ages this process was explicitly recognized and approved and the Church was seen as the heir of the Roman Empire. Even after *Romanitas* had come to have more subtle implications in theory, the fact remained that the stock on to which the cultures of mission lands were being grafted was not a neutral, timeless phenomenon, but a western culture of Graeco-Roman origin, masquerading as a world culture. As such, Christianity was contributing to the cultural imperialism of the western world.

It is interesting that St Paul, in the Epistle to the Romans, also uses the horticultural metaphor of grafting in this very connection, but his picture and his application are substantially different. The relevant passage is as follows:

> All the branches are holy if the root is holy. No doubt some of the branches have been cut off, and, like shoots of wild olive, you have been grafted among the rest to share with them the rich sap provided by the olive tree itself, but still, even if you think yourself superior to the other branches, remember that you do not support the root; it is the root that supports you. You will say, 'Those branches were cut off on purpose to let me be grafted in!' True, they were cut off, but through their unbelief; if you still hold firm, it is only thanks to your faith. Rather than making you proud, that should make you afraid. God did not spare the natural branches, and he is not likely to spare you. Do not forget that God can be severe as well as kind: he is severe to those who fell, and he is kind to you, but only for as long as he chooses to be, otherwise you will find yourself cut off too, and the Jews, if they give up their unbelief, grafted back in your place. God is perfectly able to graft them back again; after all, if you were cut off from your natural wild olive to be grafted unnaturally on to a cultivated olive, it will be much easier for them, the natural branches, to be grafted back on the tree they came from (Rom 11.16-24).

In this passage St Paul was telling the Romans that they were like a wild olive branch that had been grafted on to a cultivated olive, but the Jews were also a branch (albeit, a natural one) that had been cut off and which could, if God pleased, be re-grafted on to the tree again. St Paul pictures the many cultures as branches, all drawing the sap of life from a common root or stem. This common root is not a particular human culture, not even the Jewish culture. It is the tradition of faith in God's promises, beginning with the Patriarchs, Abraham, Isaac and Jacob, and passing through Moses to fulfilment in Christ. The first fruit of this faith was the Jewish branch, which had been cut off, and of which only a remnant was left.

The root, or stock, is therefore of a spiritual nature. It is not a culture in itself. This is the clear teaching of the Second Vatican Council. Speaking of human communities 'bound together by strong ties of cultural life, by ancient religious traditions and firm bonds of social relationships', the Council says:

> To be able to offer to all the mystery of salvation and the life brought by God, the Church must implant itself in all these groups driven by the same impulse which drove Christ, through his incarnation, to bind himself to the concrete social and cultural conditions of the people among whom he lived (*Ad Gentes,* 10).

Christ was a perfect Jew, completely identified, as we all are, with the culture into which we were born. It is the same with the Church, the sacrament of Christ. The Church has to become incarnate in each culture, re-thinking its message in the categories of the culture to which it comes. The Council envisages a stirring up of theological investigation in each major socio-cultural area so that '...it will be more clearly seen in what ways faith can seek for understanding in the philosophy and wisdom of these peoples' (*Ad Gentes,* 22). As St Paul showed, each cultural 'branch' is on a par with the others. No one branch can think it is superior to the others because: 'You do not support the root; it is the root that supports you'. The Mission is only really complete when this equality is achieved. As an African priest, Fr Meinrad Hegba wrote: 'Christian Africa will never be at home in the Church of God until she stops being under a perpetual obligation, in a condition of beggary, in a state of eternal juniority' (*Personalité Africaine et Catholicisme,* Paris n.d., p. 14).

Nevertheless, it may still be urged that a world, technological culture is a reality, and that the contemporary technological revolution makes all talk of cultural multiplicity irrelevant. The answer to this objection is that those who use it must have a very superficial understanding of the depth and tenacity of traditional cultures. Theirs is the mentality of the globe-trotter, already mentioned whose knowledge of the countries he visits is limited to the inside of expensive hotels and restaurants and to the confines of big, capital cities and international airports. Everywhere he finds the same comforts, the same menu, the same technical amenities, and he concludes that the world is a big village. Nothing could be further from the truth. Although technology may have cultural implications, it is not a culture. Unlike the Church, however, it receives its meaning from culture and has nothing to give to culture at its deepest level. Technology is neutral and has little or no cultural content. This is not to say that the introduction of a money economy, methods of communication or industrialization does not change patterns of living and behaving, or that the way in which technology is introduced into a non-western country does not owe anything to western cultural values; but it means that technology is able to serve different sets of values, and values very different from western ones.

If one analyses a person's cultural make-up, one discovers a series of levels or rings that become stronger, deeper and more impervious to change as one nears the centre. The outermost ring is superficial. It concerns a great deal of what, from a purely external and material point of view, one might call 'modern living', for example, styles of building, fashions of dress, modes of transport. Industrial techniques probably belong to this outer level, because like all the things just listed they do not affect a person very deeply and they have little to do with a person's basic cultural allegiance, his values or his philosophy of life. To discover something about a man's culture one must take a look at his home environment where he is more himself, than at his place of work. A man's cultural values have very little to do with the factory process in which he participates, or with the means he employs to go to work. These things are more or less neutral. The same is true of modern buildings and dress, which obey certain laws of efficiency, practicality, hygiene, supply, demand and availability. On the other hand, in his home life a man's domestic techniques are more his own. These are chiefly his *cuisine,* his conventions for cooking, eating, drinking, and for sleeping and spending his leisure time. Diet is much more resistant to pressures of change than dress or transportation, and the world's different culinary traditions are able to survive in their own right along with their respective table conventions in the restaurants of the most technological society. Chinese food and Chinese chop-sticks are the most obvious example.

Nevertheless, it is with the next level that we begin to approach the core of a man's cultural identity. This is the level of values. By a value we mean the priority or worth which a man gives to the phenomena of his experience, persons, things, actions. In one society distributing wealth may be a more important value than conserving wealth. In another, bearing children may be a more important value than conjugal love for its own sake. In one society generosity is a value, in others it may be success or honour. Values form a system in so far as they are interrelated, and these relationships between values are taught by society no less than the values themselves. There is a hierarchy of values, and this hierarchy in the minds of people explains their choices and their courses of action.

Finally comes the deepest level, the ultimate cultural coding of the person. This might be called the view which a society has about man and his relationship to the world, to other men, and to ultimate reality. This view of man (sometimes called 'world view') is the product of a society's response to the geographical environment which supports it and which provides it with its symbols; and it is also the fruit of a long process of internal adaptation by which individuals modify, and conform to, social patterns and structures. The view of man is thus a product of geography, economics and history. A society's values spring from this view of man, from this understanding of what it means to be a human being, and they reflect this understanding more or less successfully. The core of the view of man is a religious understanding, an area of ultimate concern, a searching for and an intuition of ultimate reality, whether or not it is expressed (as it usually is) by the worship of personalized spiritual beings. Religion, therefore, is the heart of every human culture.

Christianity (as has been said many times already) is not a culture, and it needs cultural forms in which to express itself. Nevertheless, Christianity comes to a culture to endorse and to challenge its view of man, and the values which derive from this view. After Christ there is a new view of man because God has become man, and has transformed man through the power of the Resurrection. In any view of man Christianity will find something with which to agree, something with which to disagree, because our views and our values are not adequate by themselves. They need the Gospel of Christ.

Christ challenges a culture without destroying it, or altering its essential character. This is because he challenges it from within and not from outside. Christ was completely identified with his own culture. He was so identified with it that he was not even recognized as God. It was because he was a perfect Jew that he was able to challenge the Jewish culture successfully. Christ was the perfect Jew, but he was also the universal man, and part of the challenge he offered to Jewish culture was the important teaching that no culture rests on the negative foundations of despising other cultures. A man is not more a Jew because he despises Samaritans. The definition of Englishness is not hatred for the

French or the Germans. One is not a Munyoro because one is at war with the Baganda. One is not brown or black because of a refusal to be white, or *vice versa*.

Christ, in his lifetime, went out of his way to praise the faith of people from non-Jewish cultures, the Roman centurion, the Canaanite woman, the Samaritan leper, reserving for them his most extravagant praise. In teaching the fundamental law of charity to his fellow Jews, Jesus took as his model a non-Jew, more hated and despised than any other – the Samaritan. Nothing could be more telling. Christ appealed to all cultures because he could transform them all, but he could only do this completely after the Resurrection had taken place, and he could be identified with all cultures simultaneously. The Christian knows that every view of man and every value-system is a true perspective capable of being informed and transformed by Christ. If he cannot recognize this fact, then he is unlikely to be able to recognize the transforming influence of Christ in his own culture.

The mission of the Church is the logical outcome of this recognition. Not only is it necessary to Christianize cultures if one wishes to Christianize any individual who is the product of those cultures, but it is necessary to communicate, to exchange, and to translate the Gospel of Christ from one culture to another, if one is to have a clear idea of what it means to be human and to be Christian. Without this mission and this essay in communications, one might be tempted to take Christianity for granted, as a phenomenon of one's own culture. As the mission spreads over the world to successive peoples, the richness and the depth of Christ is revealed, and with this the value of each and every human culture as yet another expression of the Christian view of man. As a result the Christian comes to a better understanding of his own culture and become more fully determined than ever to be faithful to it.

CHAPTER 8

The Universality of the Mission

Before the Second Vatican Council missionaries tended to think of the Church's catholicity in terms of baptizing as many individuals as possible. At some remote, future date the mission would be achieved when everyone in the world had had the opportunity of accepting or rejecting the Gospel of Christ. Not only is this idea difficult to reconcile with the Church's current failure to keep pace with the expanding population of the world, but, as soon as one analyses it closely one discovers that it is neither logical in itself, nor founded in Scripture. A catholicity which is only to be achieved at some remote future date is hardly very catholic. What of the countless individuals who will have died, in the meantime, without Christ being preached to them? The Church cannot succeed in preaching the Gospel to every individual in the world in any one generation, let alone in every successive generation. Two consequences follow from this premise. One is that the Church's catholicity must be socio-cultural, rather than individual. The other is that it must be symbolical, rather than literal. However, in saying that it is social, we are not saying that individuals are not our concern. Society, as we have seen, exists in the minds of individuals – but it is also something existing outside the individual and is compulsive to him, since it is the product of a collectivity of individuals. Also, in saying that the Church's catholicity is symbolical, we are not saying that it is not effective. As we shall see later, the symbol is never a bare sign; it relates to real experience.

More than this, the picture we get from the New Testament is one of the Church giving witness to socio-cultural groups – to the nations, the pagan peoples or the *Gentiles,* the *Ethnici,* the members of a *gens* or *ethnos,* a nation. The command given by Jesus was to 'make disciples of all the nations', and to 'proclaim the Good News to all creation.' It is an activity directed towards socio-cultural groups on a world-wide scale. Just as the disciples were to disperse over the inhabited world before the destruction came to Jerusalem, so an even wider world witness is to be given before the final consummation. 'This Good News of the Kingdom will be proclaimed to the whole world as a witness to all the nations. And then the end will come' (Mt 24.14). This period of world witness is the 'age of the Pagans', the era of the nations which succeeds the historical Israel.

Several texts both in the gospels and in St Paul's epistles give the impression that the Jewish nation will be the last to welcome this effective witness. Jerusalem will only rise again after the age of the pagans: 'Jerusalem will be trampled down by the pagans until the age of the pagans is completely over.' (Lk 21.24). St Paul adds the idea that the unbelief of the Jews plays a positive role in the salvation of the nations, but that their ultimate belief will be even more beneficial because it will usher in the final reconciliation and transformation of man.

> Let me put another question, then: have the Jews fallen for ever, or have they just stumbled? Obviously they have not fallen for ever: their fall, though, has saved the pagans in a way the Jews may now well emulate. Think of the extent to which the world, the pagan world, has benefited from their fall and defection – then think how much more it will benefit from the conversion of them all. Let me tell you pagans this: I have been sent to the pagans as their apostle, and I am proud of being sent, but the purpose of it is to make my own people envious of you, and in this way to save some of them. Since their rejection meant the reconciliation of the world, do you know what their admission will mean? Nothing less than a resurrection from the dead! (Rom 11.11-15).

There are two possible interpretations of these passages, a real interpretation and a metaphorical interpretation. The first would see the Jewish culture as an effective symbol in the world of the Church's unfinished task – a perpetual call to continue and to complete the mission. In this view Israel plays a role that is complementary to that of the Church, and somewhat similar to it, since it is a form of symbolic – yet effective – witness. It is essentially a witness of suffering, the greatest and most prolonged experience of suffering known to history, and it will be changed into the greatest and most glorious fulfilment at the end of time. Jewish suffering is not a consequence of collective guilt for the death of Christ. This idea has been unambiguously repudiated and strongly condemned by the Second Vatican Council (*Nostra Aetate*, 4). It is a mystery of suffering in which God himself is most surely present in the person of the Suffering Servant. Some interpreters would identify the Jewish nation, spoken of by these passages of the New Testament, as the modern State of Israel, but this would seem to be limiting the application overmuch. Jewish culture is sufficiently homogeneous in space and time and its historical continuity is sufficiently well attested for a general application of these texts to the Jews of all ages and places. The metaphorical interpretation however, would simply envisage the piece-meal integration of the Jews with the pagans to whom the Good News has been preached, a process which would culminate in the establishment of the New Jerusalem and the New Israel.

We must now face the controversial question of how the Church gives her universal witness among the pagan (non-Jewish) nations and how we are to recognize these nations. Recent controversy has been concerned with both these points. Agreed that the catholicity of the Church's mission is not a question of counting heads but of establishing a presence within differing human cultures, when can we say that this goal is achieved for any culture? This is a large question and we shall return to it, but we can, at least, assume here that it implies the conversion of a sufficient number of people to Christianity in order to ensure the moral life of the Church in that culture and the effectiveness of a community witness. It also assumes, I think, that this community is normally a growing one. The Church is therefore an effective symbol within a human culture just as it should also be an effective witness within the world as a whole.

This universal witness cannot be literal from an individual point of view; neither can it be literal from a collective point of view. By that I mean it cannot be a question of a presence in every human society that has existed or will exist. For one thing there are societies which have ceased to exist and, for another, societies which are in existence today may undergo radical changes. One much publicized opinion (that of Fr E. Hillman in *The Church as Mission,* London, 1965; and *The Wider Ecumenism,* London, 1968) holds that what Christ has done once and for all for the whole human race, the Church – in obedience to his mandate – does once and for all in each human society. The picture appears to be one of a continuous, ongoing movement, from one human society to another. One by one, and not necessarily simultaneously in one generation, the Gospel is proclaimed in each culture. In this way the witness will be given to all the nations and then the final end will come. 'This Good News of the Kingdom will be proclaimed to the whole world as a witness to all the nations. And then the end will come.' This prediction in Matthew's Gospel is not by any means nearing fulfilment, according to this view. The world is in an essentially pre-Christian, not a post-Christian, situation.

While agreeing wholeheartedly with the last statement, one must admit that the theory as a whole rests on a static view of human societies and on a too mystical, if not a metaphorical, interpretation of the Church as sacrament of the world. It is apparently assumed that human societies have an unchanging identity that continues over a long span of time, and that there should not normally be any re-evangelization of a particular society, because the Church's establishment in any society is a historical event which affects both the past and future. In fact, human societies are always changing, and at times they change so radically that their very identity is affected. This fact was clearly recognized by the Second Vatican Council.

> Moreover, the groups among which the Church dwells often undergo radical changes for one reason or another, and an entirely new set of circumstances can arise. Then the Church must deliberate whether these conditions call for a renewal of her missionary activity (*Ad Gentes,* 6).

Are we justified in appealing to the witness of a vanished Christian community or an unsuccessful mission as an excuse for not attempting to set up the Church once again as a living presence in a given human society? Should our only criterion be to proclaim the Gospel where it has not been proclaimed before? Ultimately, we come down to the question of priorities in the Church's mission. Certainly, if we are to be a Catholic Church we cannot be satisfied to be a 'western' Church or a 'white' Church, and we have the clear duty to make our proclamation of the Gospel as world-wide as possible. However, this also means taking advantage of the opportunities that are given to us and the openings that are presented for missionary activity. One cannot simply describe the incarnation of the Church in human cultures as a 'successive' process, in the sense that one turns from one culture to another in the attempt to bring each and every culture that exists, or will ever exist, to Christ. This is to make the same mistake on a collective level that was made in pre-Vatican II thinking on the level of individuals. No, our task is to try – in our time, and with the cultures of our time – to realize the symbol of the Church's catholicity, as best we can, recognizing that it is basically a symbol. The Church's universality is not a numerical or cumulative process either on a individual level or on a collective level. Moreover, our task of witness is a present task, and our catholicity is a present obligation. This means that the symbol must be real and actual in the world of today. Although it is true to say that the Church extends through time as well as space, time is not a substitute for space. We cannot appeal to the missionary activity of former ages as the basis on which to decide today's priorities.

Perhaps even more important still is the need to recognize that it is not we ourselves who decide what the priorities are, but the Holy Spirit. We have to do a certain amount of misson planning, but we must also have the faith and the understanding to see the Church's mission as a dynamic process, in which the Spirit invites, gives us new possibilities, opens up new avenues of exploration. We do not have the monopoly of the Spirit's action, and we cannot assume that the proclamation of the Gospel in a specific human community is a necessity for God in the achievement of his immediate plans for humanity. There could be no clearer example of this than St Paul's decision to evangelize Macedonia instead of Bithynia and Asia which lay in his path:

> They travelled through Phrygia and the Galatian country, having been told by the Holy Spirit not to preach the word in Asia. When they reached the frontier of Mysia they thought to cross it into Bithynia, but as the Spirit of Jesus would not allow them, they went through Mysia and came down to Troas.
> One night Paul had a vision: a Macedonian appeared and appealed to him in these words, 'Come across to Macedonia and help us.' Once he had seen the vision we lost no time in arranging a passage to Macedonia, convinced that God had called us to bring them the Good News (Acts 16.6-10).

Another flaw in the theory that the Gospel must be preached once and for all in each and every human culture is that it sees these cultures as discrete entities, each apart from the other. As a consequence it envisages an impossibly large number of cultures and makes no allowance for the convergence and the intercultural relationships to which as Catholic Christians we must be committed. Professor P. H. Gulliver's Tribal Map of mainland Tanzania lists 106 different tribal societies. Has the Gospel to be preached in each of these societies in the medium of its tribal language and culture? Are we to have 106 translations of the Bible, 106 catechisms, 106 liturgies, 106 dioceses, etc.? This is not only impossible but it runs directly counter to the programme of nation-building to which the members of all these cultures are committed. It also overlooks the fact that many of these tribal identities are extremely ephemeral. Many are composed of associations of clans and chiefdoms which command a stronger loyalty than the tribal allegiance. In many cases it is impossible to say where one tribe ends and another begins. Some political federations were only formed a few decades before the entry of the Europeans in the nineteenth century, and while one cannot go so far as to say that the colonizers actually invented the tribes, one can say that they called a halt to the dynamic process of proliferation, fission and fusion of ethnic groups. Colonization stabilized the situation, thereby laying the foundation for increased contact and exchange between the various human groups, and eventually for a modern nation-state. We cannot say that national unity has been fully achieved in the majority of cases, otherwise there would not still be talk of the need for nation-building or of the dangers of tribalism. We can still discern certain homogeneous cultural areas in which people are united by language, similar environment and similar cultural and social institutions. The Church must make itself present in these areas, catering for legitimate differences of values and expressions. At the same time she must interest herself in social institutions at the national level, secondary and higher education, universities, towns and so on. Unlike colonization which, from many points of view, created the problem of tribalism by fixing the frontiers and hardening the loyalties, the Church must continually contribute to mutual respect and understanding between cultural areas and between nations.

The Church is dedicated to contact and exchange between human cultures. We have seen that the ultimate cultural coding of the human person is extremely resistant to change, and that contact with other cultures may bring the different cultural identities more sharply into relief. It may be that the so-called tribal cultures of Asia and Africa will disappear as the culture of the Mercians and the Hwicce of Anglo-Saxon England disappeared; or they may survive in a way similar to the local loyalties of, let us say, Wales and Cornwall. Whatever is to be the outcome, we must not fall into the error of setting up a 'tribal Church'. Too often in mission countries the frontiers of dioceses have been drawn to coincide with tribal boundaries, and the tribal character of the diocese has been reinforced by missionary 'tribalism' – the confiding of a territory to missionaries of a single nationality who identify exclusively with the tribe they are evangelizing. Religious congregations have been equally tribal, and so have many other facets of the Church's life in mission lands. The result has been an inequitable distribution of local clergy and religious, and often a wastage of material resources. The tribal attitude represents a false picture of human cultures and societies; and, what is worse, it denies those who accept the Gospel the chance of being missionaries in their turn, and therefore of being truly Christian. What makes a man a missionary, and therefore a Christian, is the practical realization that Christianity is not tied to a particular culture, that it is the tradition of man's response in faith to God's promises and God's action in each and every culture. Only such a realization can contribute to the eventual reconciliation of the nations and of men in Christ, and to the unity in diversity which we call catholicity, the symbol of that ultimate reconciliation.

CHAPTER 9

Salvation and the Religions

Pre-conciliar thinking about the Church's mission was Old Testament thinking, because it gave the impression that the Church had taken over the role of the chosen race. It seemed that those who were born at the right time and place became Christians; and that they alone were the lucky ones whose salvation was assured. The salvation of the less fortunate people who were not Christians was highly precarious, if not actually impossible. This apparently capricious favouritism was difficult to reconcile with the knowledge that God desired the salvation of all men; that – as St Paul told Timothy – '(God)... wants all men to be saved and reach full knowledge of the truth' (1 Tim 2.5). If God really desired the salvation of all men, why did he make membership of a somewhat exclusive group the condition of this salvation? Why did he deny the possibility of salvation to so many people today, and in past and future ages? Such questions follow from the conclusion reached in the last chapter that the Church's catholicity is symbolic rather than literal. If, however, salvation is not the privilege of the baptized alone, we still have to ask how the symbol of catholicity is related to the reality of a salvation offered to all.

Hitherto, missionary activity was based on belief in the absolute necessity of baptism for salvation, and the Church in mission lands became a society the chief activity and aim of which was to baptize. It was held that the baptized had more opportunities for grace than non-Christians, even if grace was conceded outside the Church. The Church offered a more secure – the only secure – means of salvation. Some theologians even maintained that salvation was easier for the Christian than for the non-Christian and that the sacraments existed to make life easier. For example, the Christian could avail himself of the sacrament of penance which forgave sin without the need of perfect contrition. Imperfect contrition, or attrition, not motivated by love, was sufficient for the sacrament. The non-Christian, on the other hand, had to make an act of perfect contrition, motivated by love, if he wished to be forgiven his sins. However, not everyone accepted the opinion that a non-Christian was capable of supernatural love. Supernatural love, it was said, depended on supernatural faith, which in turn depended on an explicit knowledge of God revealed in Jesus Christ. One could take refuge in the theory dear to the Suarezians that non-Christians had a purely natural life, destined towards a goal of purely natural happiness, but that was to settle for something considerably less than a universal call by God to share in his divine life. One could not escape the conclusion that non-Christians were incapable of loving God properly, and that Christians enjoyed the privilege of not loving him, if they wanted to!

Pre-conciliar salvation theology was 'ecclesiocentric', centred on the Church, rather than theocentric, centred on God, and it was this fact which obscured the truth, never completely abandoned, that the non-Christian was capable of an implicit act of supernatural love. St Thomas Aquinas held that if a man 'directs himself to his due end, he will, by means of grace, receive the remission of original sin' (1a 2ae, 89, in c.). The Council of Trent taught that baptism could be received by desire, and this led to the development of the theology of the *votum, desiderium* or *propositum sacramenti*. On the one hand the Church from very early times maintained the axiom: *extra ecclesiam nulla salus,* 'outside the Church there is no salvation', but on the other, she condemned the Jansenist proposition: *extra ecclesiam nulla conceditur gratia,* 'outside the Church there is no grace'. How was one to resolve this apparent contradiction? Was there salvation or not outside the Church? The Church is the Body of Christ; might it not be truer to say that there is no salvation outside of Christ? This would be a good escape from the *impasse* were it not that we still need to know how the Church is related to salvation outside her visible boundaries, and also just how salvation through Christ can operate without an explicit acknowledgment of him.

In general, the answer being given to the first question is that there is no salvation 'without the Church', that, even though there be no visible link with the Church, the Church is intimately and essentially related to the process by which non-Christians are saved. However, in order to answer this question in detail, we must first deal with the second question of the salvation of individual non-Christians.

We have seen that, according to St Thomas Aquinas, a man can 'direct himself to his due end'. This is to make a fundamental option in life under the influence of grace. It is commonly taught today that such an option is by necessity an implicit act of faith and charity. One who has made it is living in a state of grace and has what is commonly called 'the baptism of desire'. The option that a man makes is a fundamental choice between two alternatives either to place himself first or last as the object of ultimate concern. If he places that ultimate concern outside himself, he is orientated towards God. There cannot be a natural or neutral state; one must choose between God and self. God created mankind for supernatural life, and human sin has not made any difference to that decision. We are still called by God to that supernatural end. The whole of creation is called to fulfilment in Christ; and God inclines it to that end through grace, his dynamic influence and presence. A man can therefore only accept or reject this invitation and this orientation.

This option is made at the deepest level of personal commitment. It is not necessarily something of which we are normally conscious, but it integrates and animates all our actions. If we stand back and reflect about our lives we should be able to discover whether the mainspring of our life is genuine love or selfishness, avidity and pride. The fundamental option in faith and charity finds expression first of all in a personal creed. This is the expression of the option in a religious attitude or way of life; in verbal form, through abstract formulations or through literary symbols; and in ritual form or forms of symbolic action or worship. We have already seen that a man is largely a product of the society to which he belongs; it is normal, therefore, that his personal creed should be profoundly influenced by the values and moral ideals presented to him in the corporate creed of his society. Before the Second Vatican Council the missionary tended to imagine he was dealing with isolated individuals. While it is perfectly true that society exists in the minds of individuals and that individuals, not social facts, are confronted by the call of Christ, it is equally true that the individual cannot be evangelized without reference to other individuals and without reference to the social order which an aggregation of individuals necessarily generates. The next question to ask is whether these social facts are a help or a hindrance in the formation of a man's personal creed. Are non-Christians saved because of, or in spite of, their non-Christian religious traditions?

The answer to this question is already implicit in all that has been said about man and his culture. It is altogether unreasonable to imagine that a man should work out his salvation by separating himself from his culture, especially when Christianity itself is obliged to identify itself with human cultures. If a man in the pre-Christian situation is expected to work out his salvation, it must be in and through the culture to which he belongs; and it must be assumed that his culture and the religious traditions of that culture play a positive role in helping him to formulate his personal creed. From this it follows that God actually uses these non-Christian religious traditions as instruments for bringing salvation to men, while tolerating the imperfections that they contain. St Paul, speaking before the Council of the Areopagus, was very clear on this point. Until Christ was preached and men ceased to be ignorant of the full knowledge of the truth, God actually sanctioned their social order and their efforts at finding him. What is more, he overlooked their religious deviations:

> From one single stock he not only created the whole human race so that they could occupy the entire earth, but he also decreed how long each nation should flourish and what the boundaries of its territory should be. And he did this so that all nations might seek the deity and, by feeling their way towards him, succeed in find-

ing him. Yet in fact he is not far from any of us, since it is in him that we live and move and exist, as indeed some of your own writers have said:

'We are all his children'.

Since we are the children of God, we have no excuse for thinking that the deity looks like anything in gold, silver or stone that has been carved and designed by a man.

God overlooked that sort of thing when men were ignorant, but now he is telling everyone everywhere that they must repent, because he has fixed a day when the whole world will be judged, and judged in righteousness, and he has appointed a man to be the judge. And God has publicly proved this by raising this man from the dead (Acts 17.26-31).

The preaching of Christ in any society is a historical event which is a direct challenge to the religious tradition of that society, but is also, and more especially, a fulfilment of the tradition. Non-Christian religions are not to be seen as essentially false, but rather as incomplete, as a matter of fact. Since the Church is the servant of all who acknowledge God, she has the duty to recognize the activity of the Holy Spirit even when it takes place outside her visible boundaries. This is an important part of the Church's prophetic task. We cannot presume that God's action is circumscribed by the limitations of the Church, and we must be ready to discern that action whenever and wherever it occurs, to point it out, and even to make it our own. We should even believe that God may allow non-Christians to take initiatives, to develop insights, and pursue moral goods which can enrich historical Christianity when they are brought into contact with it. God may have permitted these insights as an anticipation of future Christian developments. The Vatican Council exhorts Christians, not merely to acknowledge, but also to preserve and promote, the moral goods found in non-Christian religious traditions:

The Church therefore has this exhortation for her sons: prudently and lovingly, through dialogue and collaboration with the followers of other religions, and in witness of Christian faith and life, to acknowledge, preserve, and promote the spiritual and moral goods found among these men, as well as the values in their society and culture (*Nostra Aetate,* 2).

Such an exhortation implies serious study of non-Christian religions and dialogue with those who profess them. It excludes intolerance, discrimination and contempt. The Christian might be more impressed by the worship and the splendid buildings of the so-called world religions than he is by the diversity, poverty and obscurity of the so-called primitive religions; but he is not at liberty to make unfavourable comparisons between them. Primitive religions are systems of ideas and moral values which are often highly developed because they are less encumbered by the materiality of temples and elaborate worship. Basically, religions cannot be compared as systems. Not only do religions, as Fr Schlette points out (H.R. Schlette, *Towards a Theology of Religions,* London 1965, p. 52), have an absolute character which defies scientific comparison, but all are vehicles of salvation in the Christian view, and all, as we shall see, have a place in the ultimate convergence to which Christianity is the explicit witness. The superiority of Christianity over other religions is not founded on a process of despising them or discriminating against them. It is not even founded on a present adverse judgement about the measure of error or falsity which they contain. The more we despise non-Christian religions, the less right we have to feel superior to them. Christianity's superiority consists simply in the fact that it points to the culmination of a historical process of which all these religions are a part.

Christians, however, cannot claim that they know what shape this culmination will take. They do not know how far it will be realized in history; nor do they know what repercussions the convergence of religions will have on the Christianity which they know today. Other religions are incomplete, but so is Christianity until Christ fills all, and God is 'all in all'. Christians cannot even deny to other religions a glimpse of the culmination to which they themselves give witness; nor can they refuse to recognize the signs that they are tending towards this convergence. On the contrary, the profession of their faith demands that they give this recognition and look for these signs.

This does not, by any means, imply a religious relativism. We are dealing ultimately with individuals and not with disembodied social facts. Religion is essentially a personal affair and concerns the confrontation of persons – individuals in society. What matters is that a man follows his conscience; and that he conscientiously adheres to what he deems to be the truth. To say that all religions are salutary is not at all to say that it doesn't matter what religion one belongs to. On the contrary, it matters very much, for the personal creed consists in making a corporate creed one's own, and this precludes the possibility of indifference towards one's corporate creed.

The different religions of the world are not even agreed on the diagnosis of the world's ills, let alone on the remedies prescribed to cure them, and it is fruitless to speak as if they are comparable. It is also fruitless to assume that one can disengage the salutary element in non-Christian religions, as if it were a nucleus capable of development into something called Christianity. By themselves these religions will not develop into Christianity any more than Old Testament Israel could have developed by itself into the Church of the New Testament. These religions have to be challenged by the person of Jesus Christ either explicitly or implicitly, but always from within the tradition. Either Christ is proclaimed through the agency of the Church which recognizes what the Second Vatican Council has called the authentic 'seeds of the gospel' in the non-Christian tradition, and which incarnates itself within the religious culture; or else the Spirit of Christ operates anonymously within the non-Christian tradition, confronting it with an ever clearer vision of how human expectations are to be fulfilled. It follows that what Christians are doing by their corporate witness in the world is bound up with the salvation of non-Christians, and that all religions are orientated towards what the Church represents and what she is trying explicitly to bring about. All salutary acts, inside or outside the Church, are related to the Incarnation and Paschal Mystery of Christ and all of this will be acknowledged when the non-Christian religions take their rightful place in the Church of the future, the spotless spouse of the Lamb of God.

CHAPTER 10

Priorities in the Mission

In an article, 'Starvation by 1980' (R. H. Fuller and B. K. Rice: *Christianity and the Affluent Society,* London 1966), the Reverend Brian Rice gave a graphic illustration of the unfair distribution of resources in the world. If one reduced the population of the world proportionately to that of a single town containing 1,000 people, one would find only 303 white people, but 697 non-whites. Out of the town's inhabitants 60 would be Americans and 16 would be British. Together they would receive more than half the income of the entire town and they would eat 72% above the food requirements of the rest of the town.

In such a town there would be 330 Christians of all denominations, and of these some 165 would be Roman Catholics. Carrying Rice's metaphor still further, one could calculate that out of the 165 Roman Catholics about 100 would be white Americans and Europeans. These white Roman Catholics, whether practising or lapsed, would have at their disposition the services of the vast majority of the Church's personnel. Rice's sample is too small to show the proportion of clergy to laity among the Roman Catholics of his world town, but there are only some 400,000 priests in the whole world, and of these only 30,000 work in non-western countries. This means that in Europe and North America there is one priest for every 800 Catholics, but in the rest of the world one priest for every 6,500 Catholics. No other conclusion is possible but that the Roman Catholic Church is identified with the rich, white minority of the world, that it is a predominantly western Church and that its resources and personnel are concentrated in such a way as to perpetuate the westernness of the Church. This may be an accident of history, but it is not a fact about which we can be complacent in the context of the world mission of the Church today.

A Church which is predominantly western naturally thinks western. Its scholars and theologians are westerners, absorbed by western problems. For example, the Church's theology of marriage is so interwoven with the outlook of Roman law and so bound up with western social institutions that western missionaries can make little or no headway in Christianizing the social institutions of Africa and Asia. Marriage and family systems in Africa and Asia appear to have no coherence of their own, but appear only as so many infractions of a law made in Europe. Again, people in the so-called mission countries can now worship in the vernacular, but the texts they are obliged to use are translations from an original composed in Europe, in a European language, a text which owes nothing to their own categories of thought and their own traditions of worhsip. By and large, Africa and Asia do not have their own devotional practices, their own religious congregations, their own forms of lay apostolate. Apart from a few exceptions, all these things are devised in Europe and come from Europe. The missionary congregations who evangelize Africa and Asia have their mother-houses in Europe and America, and it is there that decisions affecting Africa and Asia are taken. If people in Africa and Asia want information about their own Churches, they must turn to information services created in Europe and America. Students are sent to Europe and America to places of learning and it is from the ranks of these that Church leaders are chosen. While admitting the indispensable role played by western missionaries and the continuing need for assistance from Europe, the Churches of Africa and Asia must say with Cardinal Zoungrana (in his address to the Second Symposium of Episcopal Conferences of Africa and Madagascar, Abidjan, August 19th 1970): 'Our very being must not be conferred upon us from outside.'

Part of the problem, it is true, is the very strongly centralized character of Latin Christianity. We spoke always of the 'Western Church' in contrast to the 'Eastern Churches' or the 'Uniate Churches'. Church traditions, rites, and theological emphases are tied to an ethno-political base. In the West, the Roman Empire was the overriding political and cultural fact. In the East the evolution was more complex. However, even in the West, the Celtic and Germanic cultures did not succumb without a struggle. With how much less justice should the Churches of Africa and Asia be called 'western'? With how much less justice should they be deemed a single regional Church?

The Second Vatican Council has encouraged a greater degree of pluralism in Latin Christianity, and much is said by the Council Fathers about 'particular churches' or 'local churches'; but even if it is assumed that the local churches in so-called mission lands are due to reach their maturity and to aquire their own character and a limited autonomy, it is difficult to see how this can be achieved with the present western stranglehold on the Church in mission countries. Moreover, with the failure to produce an indigenous clergy in adequate numbers, it is difficult to see the Church expanding to make herself present in more and more non-Christian cultures. Priests and religious are too busy ministering to the needs of the already baptized. More than this, they are actually losing ground.

Europe and North America are becoming post-Christian,

and since Abbé Godin called France 'a mission country', the word 'mission' has been increasingly applied to western countries in a post-Christian situation. This usage has been vigorously attacked by Fr Eugene Hillman, C.S.Sp. (E. Hillman: *The Church as Mission,* London 1966), who argues that this is a pastoral, rather than a missionary, problem. His definition of mission restricts it to the preaching of the Gospel for the first time in a nation or culture. Only the early stages of establishing a Christian community, he believes, can be strictly called missionary. After that, all is pastoral work, the servicing of an already existing community. This is a thoroughly pre-conciliar view, pre-conciliar because it plays down the missionary character of the Church as a whole, and of its total action. Many missiologists have defined the missionary task of the Church as that of 'planting' or 'building' the Church in a non-Christian country, but there was no criterion by which it could be decided when the mission church had come of age. When was the misson church mature? When it had its own diocesan hierarchy? When it no longer depended on foreign personnel and foreign resources? When it was no longer responsible to the Sacred Congregation for Evangelizing Peoples? If these are the criteria, then the mission churches are doomed to a long – not to say, an eternal – state of immaturity. There never has been any official act of recognition, any independence ceremony by which a mission church was seen to have come of age. Indeed, one might ask: 'Should one ever think that a church is mature? Is not the task of building a church an endless process, because of shifting social currents, new moral problems, and developing cultures? Are there not always new commitments and new expenses, and should there not be a continual exchange between the Churches? Is this not, ultimately, what 'communion' entails?'

All of this is true, but there is an obvious difference between the time when a viable, living Christian community exists and the time when it does not. One must agree with Fr Hillman that there is a necessary, early stage in which the Gospel is being preached for the first time and the first adherents are being assembled, but one must avoid labelling this period 'missionary' in contradistinction to any later period of Christian activity. After all, one could justifiably say that it is only when the Christian community has come into existence that real missionary activity begins. Christian witness is essentially a community witness. Priests and missionaries who are integrated in their communities are not doing merely pastoral work. Their task, it is true, is principally directed towards community formation through Word and Sacrament, but all of this is in view of the task of the whole community – that of the mission to the world in general, and of the mission to their own society and culture in particular. Pope Paul VI could say to the people of Africa in 1969: 'You are now missionaries to yourselves.'

The mission of the Church should not be viewed in terms of one dimension only, expansion in space. There is also the dimension of penetration and adaptation over a period of time. As we have seen, cultures are far from static. New philosophies, new moral ideals and problems come into existence with all of which the Church must grapple – the so-called 'permissive society', organic transplants, the contraceptive pill, racial discrimination and so on. The actual physical composition of the so-called 'Christian nations' can change radically. The failure of the Church to adapt its structures in time may result in a whole generation coming into existence which is ignorant of Christ. This happened in Europe when the Churches ignored the new industrial conglomerations of the nineteenth century. Or again, massive immigration from non-Christian countries, and the growing cosmopolitan character of cities and industrial areas may also radically change the situation, as it is now doing in parts of Europe. Christian communities are continually being challenged by new situations and the mission of the Church to the world must never stop.

In the so-called mission countries Christian communities are faced with the same task of penetration. Primarily it is the problem of communicating the riches of Christianity expressed in one cultural form to people from another culture. This is not something which can be achieved in one generation only. The early stages of the mission are concerned with the formation of a first nucleus of neophytes. The faith they acquire is expressed largely in therms of the missionary's own culture. The missionary, however, has to learn something of the culture of the people to whom he is preaching, otherwise verbal communication is impossible, the first hymns and catechisms are not literary classics; one finds in them such linguistic monstrosities as *kumerita grasiya* ('to merit grace'), but somehow the Christian spirit catches on. It is more through a kind of osmosis, than any conscious action, that adaptation takes place. Christianity rubs off one culture on to another, transforming it in the process. The missionary does not suspend operations while he carries out an anthropological survey of the people he plans to evangelize; that would be merely delaying the process of penetration. However, he is not absolved of conscious reflection and of an ever more thorough attempt to understand the new culture, to think and speak in its categories. By contrast the first generation of indigenous priests, teachers and Christians have the obligation to try and understand the culture of the missionary in order to get at the essential Christian message contained in it. A disembodied Christianity is an impossibility, and so both missionary and indigenous Christian must be bridge-men, men of two cultures. As time goes on on, however, indigenous priests and Christians will feel freer to think, speak about and act on their Christianity purely in terms of their own culture. This may take several generations.

Still, it is only the beginning of their mission. The indigenous Church has to face all manner of moral problems and secular ideals and to understand how these are to be confronted by Christ. Tribalism, the inferior status of women, xenophobic nationalism, material and social development and so on. The missionary age of a church does not end with the faulty translation of a catechism or hymn-book.

That being said, we can see that the imbalance between the western and non-western churches cannot be discussed in terms of pastoral work versus mission work, or of the mature church versus the missionary church. It is a question of deciding what the mission priorities are in the context of the Church's total mission to the world. If the vast majority of the world's Christians are white, then it is normal for the majority of the world's priests to be white; but we still have to ask whether it is normal in a Church calling itself 'universal' for the majority of Christians to be white. The answer is that it is not normal and that there is something wrong with our catholicity. We are, however, at least pledged to a catholic ideal, and to live up to the name of Catholic it is imperative that we make efforts to set the imbalance right. The Church has to be an effective symbol of universal reconciliation.

We have already seen that Catholicity is not a numerical or a cumulative process. Western nations with denser populations have a right to larger Christian communities. Perhaps also, the rapidity of technological change which they are experiencing poses more numerous and larger problems which rightly absorb more missionary energy, but the fact still remains that the western influence is a dead weight in the non-western churches, impeding indigenization. Even when the enlightened western missionary or the enlightened indigenous priest vindicates the right of the missionary churches to a greater freedom and autonomy, it is often a vindication of the right to be more western than the western churches themselves and to see in the forces of renewal and diversification coming from Europe and North America a new and subtle form of western domination. Renewal must come from within the non-western churches, and not from the west. Priests and missionaries have to act as catalysts, rather than as wreckers or builders, stimulating indigenization and renewal.

The Church in the west cannot force anything on the non-western churches. It cannot even force indigenization, because a forced indigenization is not a valid indigenization. Recently there has been talk among missionaries of the need to 'phase out' of mission countries. The idea was partly due to a desire to help the indigenous Christians find their own feet and acquire self-reliance and self-confidence. It was also partly due to a disillusionment of missionaries with what they deem 'the ingratitude of the people'. The missionaries are foreigners, and more and more their contributions are belittled and their presence made unwelcome. Phasing out could be interpreted as clearing out when things get bad – clearing out with a final slap in the face and a final slam of the door. The missionary's work is not meant to be easy, and if the continued presence of missionaries involves hardship for them, that has to be seen in the perspective of Christ's passion, the passion of the first missionary, who did not run away. The non-western churches are opposed to phasing out, and it is for the indigenous clergy and laity to take the decision about the continued service of missionaries. What is needed, it has been said, it not so much 'phasing out' as 'phasing in' – a phasing into structures and programmes which are essentially indigenous and ultimately non-western. After all, exchange and communion are still possible even after the de-westernization of the missionary-churches. Indigenization means an integral relationship of the Christian message to the concern experienced by people in a given society about their destiny and the destiny of the human race. It is not a matter of buildings, school uniforms, printing presses, literacy and hygiene. It is not even a matter of the presence or absence of foreign missionaries. It is an attitude of mind.

CHAPTER 11

Neo-colonialism in the Church?

Neo-colonialism is best described in the words of the old adage: 'He who pays the piper calls the tune.' Neo-colonialism is the situation whereby the former colonial powers are still able to manipulate the policies and, ultimately, the destinies of their former colonies, because they hold the purse-strings. The ex-colonial mother-countries have highly diversified, industrial economies, and this gives them resilience to meet successive economic crises. The developing ex-colony, on the other hand, produces a relatively small number of raw materials for the markets of the former colonial countries. It is the latter who fix the market price to their own advantage with the result that the poor nations remain ever poor while the rich can become still richer.

Aid for development and capital investment in developing countries are, as everyone knows, far from disinterested. They are, of course, 'gifts with strings'. The strings may not be immediately visible, but they are there. The gifts are made in order to obtain strategic or diplomatic advantages, if not crudely material ones. Through such aid ex-colonial powers are able to influence the political decisions of developing countries. The recipient, in any case, must choose to accept or refuse the gift that is offered. He may have little choice as to what is offered and under what conditions it is to be used. This is neo-colonialism.

Neo-colonialism was very strongly and very clearly condemned by Pope Paul VI in what was perhaps the greatest document of his pontificate, *Populorum Progressio:*

> ...the receiving countries could demand that there be no interference in the political life or subversion of their social structures. As sovereign states they have the right to conduct their own affairs, to decide on their own policies and to move freely towards the kind of society they choose. What must be brought about, therefore, is a system of co-operation freely undertaken, an effective and mutal sharing, carried out with equal dignity on either side, for the construction of a more human world (*Populorum Progressio*, 54).

Forty years ago Pope Pius XI in *Quadragesimo Anno* enunciated the principle of subsidiarity in which he condemned the practice of higher social bodies taking over functions which could easily be performed by bodies at a lower social level. This he described as 'a gravely harmful disturbance of right order'. At the time of the Second Vatican Council there were many voices demanding that the Church should apply its principle of subsidiarity to its own structures, and that unnecessary centralization should be abandoned. Has not the time come to ask that the Church's condemnation of neo-colonialism be applied to its own financial practice?

The fact is that as much as 80% of the Church's total income in a so-called mission country may come from outside sources. The proportion which comes from Rome itself is actually not so high. Much more comes via the various missionary institutes, the private contributions of missionary priests, and begging trips organized by the dioceses. Attached to the overseas grants are often very stringent conditions. Often, too, the money is never transferred, but is administered by the overseas agencies themselves. When one considers what the money is spent on, one finds a very high expenditure on buildings, and comparatively little in the way of funds for the training and security of personnel. The missionary Church is very rich in buildings and very poor in liquid cash. This perpetuates the economic serfdom of the Church in developing countries. The operating expenses of the Church are so high in these poor countries that it is impossible for it to break free from the bonds which shackle it to the west; and as long as these bonds are there, African and Asian Christians are not masters in their own house. The degree of dependence on decisions taken in Rome or in other cities of Europe and America are often in direct ratio to the proportion of the budget which comes from overseas.

This is not a question of cynicism or bad will on the part of Christians in the western world. We are all victims of a system. As Rev. T. A. Beetham (*Christianity and the New Africa,* London 1967, pp. 30-31) writes:

> However much mutual trust is developed, however genuine the concern of the giving body to divest itself of this remote control, its responsibility in moral stewardship or in legal trust to the subscribers who contribute the money usually makes it impossible to write a blank cheque. This is the problem of neo-colonialism in the Church; it is a problem of stewardship and fellowship, of learning how to give and how to receive. It calls for deeper understanding and trust

on both sides, as the words of St Vincent de Paul to his novices suggest: 'It is for your love and that alone that men will pardon you for the bread you give them.'

Comparing the Church to a colonial power is not completely fair, since the relationship of local churches to each other, and in particular to the local church of Rome, whose bishop holds the primacy of jurisdiction in all the churches that make up the Church Universal, is not a question of witholding or granting independent status. The local churches are in communion with each other and the collegiality of their bishops signifies a collective responsibility for the whole Church and every part of it. The relationship is, or should be, one of mutal love, trust and respect. The fact that the Church is an international communion requires that there be a minimum of international structure. For this reason the Church maintains a worldwide diplomatic service which performs a very useful task of co-ordination, helping also to ensure the freedom of action of the local churches. There are two current criticisms made of papal nuncios in developing countries, and while they are valid criticisms, the Church herself is not entirely to blame. One criticism is that the papal diplomatic service involves too much expenditure and that the multiplication of palatial nunciatures and expensive cars are a waste as well as a scandal in poor countries. The other criticism is that nuncios interfere far too much in the local church's running of its own affairs and inhibit initiative. The multiplication of nunciatures, however, is partly due to the multiple grants of independence to so many former colonies each of which demands a full diplomatic corps, and the interference of nuncios in local church affairs is partly due to the fact that these same countries see in the nuncio a spokesman of the Church who is more powerful than the local hierarchy. In spite of this, it might be possible to amalgamate delegations to coincide with the larger political and economic groupings of developing countries, to reduce unnecessary expenditure and to make a determined effort to recruit local men for the papal diplomatic service.

It is obviously true that financial self-reliance is the only ultimate condition for local autonomy, but there can be few bishops in developing countries who have the courage to refuse a grant from overseas so as to retain their independence. To cut off overseas aid now would mean the end of the Church in these countries. As Fr Theo Van Asten W.F.

told the Bishops of Africa at Abidjan in August 1970,

> ...to cut off external support for the sake of a recognized need for self-reliance would be missionary suicide. Self-reliance is fundamental but it cannot be the king-pin of development. It is, if you like, a strategic objective; to make it a tactical necessity would be to deny in a way the solidarity of the universal Church with your own national or continental Church.

One example of an attempt to be self-reliant too early was that of the Anglican Communion in Uganda. The Church of Uganda set out to keep the three 'selfs': to be self-supporting, self-governing and self-propagating. However, the last two objectives were rendered more remote by the failure to achieve immediately the first. Funds were not forthcoming for the adequate training of local ministers who could eventually take the reins of church government into their own hands. The Church in developing countries is still very much in need of help, however much its operating expenses may be rationalized.

However, it is not only a question of the poorer local churches still needing help; it is also a question of the richer local churches exercising good stewardship in their affluence and being under a heavy obligation to help their poorer brothers. The Second Vatican Council had this to say on the subject:

> As for the advanced nations, they have a very heavy obligation to help the developing people in the discharge of the aforementioned responsibilities (seeking complete human fulfilment and cultivating their own resources). If this worldwide collaboration is to be established, certain psychological and material adjustments will be needed among the advanced nations and should be brought about. Thus these nations should carefully consider the welfare of weaker and poorer nations when negotiating with them (*Gaudium et Spes,* 86).

More specifically for the income of the poorer churches, the Vatican Council addressed itself to the bishops of the affluent nations:

> They should deal with the definite offering which in proportion to its resources each diocese is obliged to set aside annually for the work of the missions. They should consider how to direct and organize the ways and means by which the missions receive direct help *(Ad Gentes,* 38).

There is nothing new in affluent churches helping poorer ones. The custom is as old as the very origins of the Church, for St Paul's epistles to the Corinthians and to the Romans contain quite a few references to the collection that he was making for the poor of the Jerusalem church. St Paul gave the Corinthians many reasons why they should be generous. Some of the reasons were very human indeed. He spurred them on with reports of the generosity of churches which, like that of Macedonia, were poorer than their own church at Corinth. He taunted them with the prospect of failing to complete the project they had begun. He begged them not to give the lie to the boasts he had made about Corinthian generosity. However, his most important arguments were theological. 'Remember how generous the Lord Jesus was: he was rich, but he became poor for your sake, to make you rich out of his poverty' (2 Cor 8.9). In other words, riches are a charism from the Holy Spirit; and they are given to us to help make others rich spiritually, just as Jesus chose poverty in order to enrich us spiritually. Again, 'the one who provides seed for the sower and bread for food will provide you with all the seed you want and make the harvest of your good deeds a larger one, and made richer in every way, you will be able to do all the generous things which, through us, are the cause of thanksgiving to God' (2 Cor 9.1-11). Almsgiving to the poorer churches is like sowing a seed; it brings an even greater harvest of generosity. Notice that there is no selfish *quid pro quo* envisaged here; generosity begets generosity which is its own reward. To these reasons St Paul adds another: the Corinthians' generosity will increase the amount of thanksgiving which God receives, because the Christians of Jerusalem will thank God all the more when they learn of the charity of the Church of Corinth. To the Romans St Paul wrote :'It is really repaying a debt: the pagans who share the spiritual possessions of these poor people have a duty to help them with their temporal possessions' (Rom 15.27). Just as we share spiritual goods between the Churches, we are under an obligation to share material goods also.

Perhaps the most important reason which St Paul adduces is this interdependence between the churches. It is a question, as he says, of balancing:

> 'This does not mean that to give relief to others you ought to make things difficult: it is a question of balancing what happens to be your surplus now against their present need, and one day they may have some-

thing to spare that will supply your own need. That is how we strike a balance: as scripture says: The man who gathered much had none too much, the man who gathered little did not go short' (2 Cor 8.13-15).

This idea of interdependence between the churches was carried still further by the Second Vatican Council and the need for balancing material resources was related to the missionary character of the Church itself.

> The grace of renewal cannot flourish in communities unless each of them extends the range of its charity to the ends of the earth, and devotes to those far off a concern similar to that which it bestows on those who are its own members. Thus the whole community prays, collaborates, and exercises activity among the nations through those of its sons whom God chooses for this most excellent task.
>
> Provided the universal scope of mission work is not thereby neglected, it will be very useful for a community to maintain contact with missionaries who came from its ranks, or with some parish or diocese in the missions. In this way the bond between the communities will be made visible, and will provide mutual edification (*Ad Gentes,* 37).

Finally St Paul has something to say about the manner of collecting for the missions:

> Every Sunday, each one of you must put aside what he can afford, so that collections need not be made after I have come. When I am with you, I will send your offering to Jerusalem by the hand of whatever men you give letters to; if it seems worthwhile for me to go too, they can travel with me (1 Cor 16.1-4).

St Paul is here recommending to the Corinthians that their giving should be proportionate to what they earn and can afford. The giving is also to be regular, every Sunday – not just on one Sunday of the year. It is the duty of each and every Christian and it is to be performed in the home. The offerings are not to be brought to church. It is only when Paul himself comes that the money will be put together and carried to Jerusalem. Needless to say, we are very far from this ideal in the Church today; we do not have regular contributions for the missions. Instead, missionaries are obliged to organize appeals and begging trips, or to rely on annual collections; and yet, if it is true that the Church and every member of the Church is essentially missionary, there should be regular, total support for the missions.

The poorer local churches are in need of help; but they are also in need of help to help themselves. The magnificent buildings and standard of living of the clergy in these countries may have discouraged generosity among the faithful. So may have the paternalism of the missionaries. Yet it is still a fact that the people are poor and cannot make much of a contribution towards the high operating costs of their church. The Church has to help them create the wealth out of which they can make their own contributions and support their own institutions. It is no use asking for money which does not exist. President Nyerere of Tanzania wrote in his Arusha Declaration:

> The development of a country is brought about by people, not by money. Money and the wealth it represents is the result and not the basis of development (J. K. Nyerere: *Ujamaa,* Oxford 1968, pp. 28-9).

The Church, therefore, has the obligation to co-operate in material development, not merely by gifts, loans and relief work, but also by her members participating in development and co-operative schemes and by putting her full weight behind such schemes when they are launched by the government. If the Church is seen to be concerned with the material advancement of her people – especially if bishops, priests and sisters give practical examples of this concern – then individual Christians will be materially concerned about their Church, and about the support of their pastors.

CHAPTER 12

The Mission: Human Communication in a Secular Age

Modern theologians, grappling with the problem of secularism, are often poor anthropologists, and one of the more astonishing by-products of their secular theology is their easy acceptance of the naive evolutionist schemes of nineteenth-century anthropologists and sociologists, such as Fustel de Coulanges, Comte and Spencer. In these schemes one nearly always finds three stages, and the theologians faithfully reproduce them. One of the crudest is that of Harvey Cox (Harvey Cox: *The Secular City,* London 1965), where the evolution is from tribe to town, and from town to technopolis. The caricature is scarcely credible. The religion of the tribe is one of 'ghosts' and 'demons' and of an awe for natural phenomena. The people in the tribal situation deify nature and impute a magical power to natural objects. By contrast, the religion of the town is one of 'gods' who are the symbols of social groups; religious belief is socially structured and metaphysical. The technopolis, finally, provides the setting for people who have no need of religion, but who are entirely absorbed in dominating their environment through technological progresss. The tribe indulges in a crude collectivism in which the individial is a kind of robot, at the mercy of immutable traditions. He is hardly a personal 'self'. He does not so much live in the tribe, but the tribe lives in him. In the town, however, individuation is present, but personal relationships are highly structured and authoritarian. Finally, in the technopolis partnership and teamwork between equals become possible.

Although Harvey Cox, like the old-fashioned evolutionists, is prepared to blur the lines of demarcation between the three stages and say that the town is partly tribe, and the technopolis partly town, there is not an anthropologist living who would accept the validity of his three stages. We discussed the question of collectivism and individualism in tribal societies in Chapter Six. In the matter of religious belief, it is an absurdity to dismiss the religion of tribal societies as one of belief in ghosts and demons. Their religions can be as 'metaphysical' and as highly structured as the religion described for the town. They do not have an awe before nature which makes them deify it. On the contrary, in many cases they seek to dominate their environment through a balanced view of the sacred. Harvey Cox misunderstands the nature of magic. It is not religion, but an essentially secular phenomenon by which men in tribal societies, like the scientists of the modern technological age, imagine that they can dominate their environment without the necessity of direct reference to God. However, even magic, erroneous as is its theory in scientific terms, is compatible with true religious belief. Magic is considered part of God's creation, and, as the rain-doctor explained to David Livingstone, God is the cause of rain just as he is the cause of medical cures, and yet both rain-doctor and medical doctor take the credit for what God does! (David Livingstone: *Missionary Travels and Researches,* London 1857). The truth is that both Livingstone and Harvey Cox were too prejudiced by their experience of secularism to be able to recognize the integration of sacred and secular when they saw it. They started from the position in which God is a 'God of the gaps', retreating before man's ingenuity. Controlling the rain is still largely beyond man's powers, and therefore it is God's province. The evolutionist theologian cannot admit the integration of sacred and secular as a historic fact; for him it must be the future culmination of his evolutionary system. His mistake lies in projecting back into history, and out into other cultures, the separation between sacred and secular which characterizes his modern, western world.

Sacred and secular are not opposite poles; they are relative aspects of the same reality. The sacred represents order and meaning, wholeness and harmony. The secular represents the technical to which the sacred gives meaning. The sacred is ultimate reality and its opposite is symbolized by 'uncleanness', disorder and sin which can be brought about by a sacral, as well as a secularist situation. The sacral mentality, no less than the secularist, is a flight from reality; both involve the separation of sacred and secular. In previous ages the temptation has been to follow the sacral aberration; in the recent history of the west the aberration has been the secularist variety. These facts, however, do not disprove the historical existence of societies in which people with an albeit limited view of the sacred have achieved a successful synthesis with a secular, but undeveloped, technology.

Symbolism, which is a form of conventional signification that is grounded in natural signs, is indispensable for an integrated view of reality and for giving value and meaning to the technical. Symbolism is the only method of communication possible when persons wish to reveal themselves to each other, because symbolism is semi-incarnate in experience and employs the very life-processes of which we are conscious as part of ourselves, eating, drinking, touching, seeing, sexuality etc. Symbolism alone is able to humanize and render intelligible the phenomena of the world in which we live, the world which we ourselves – in partnership with the Creator – are building and perfecting. The modern secular theologian, however, turns his back on symbolism because he associates it with a sacral mentality, and the sacral is for him essentially an unscientific mentality. My contention is that symbolism is not the consequence of imperfect or undeveloped science. Symbolism refers to real experience, and the power of symbolic reference in this experience does not derive from the fact that an erroneous or unscientific hypothesis is offered in explanation of the experience. Jospeh Wood Krutch has put this very well:

> The table before which we sit may be, as the scientist maintains, composed of dancing atoms, but it does not reveal itself to us as anything of the kind, and it is not with dancing atoms but a solid motionless object that we live. So remote is this 'real' table – and most of the other 'realities' with which science deals – that it cannot be discussed in terms which have any human value, and though it may receive our purely intellectual credence, it cannot be woven into the pattern of life as it is led, in contradistinction to life as we attempt to think about it. Vibrations in the ether are so totally unlike, let us say, the colour purple that the gulf between them cannot be bridged, and they are, to all intents and purposes, not one but two separate things of which the second and less real must be the most significant for us. And just as the sensation which has led us to attribute an objective reality to a non-existent thing which we call 'purple' is more important for human life than the conception of vibration of a certain frequency, so too the belief in God, however ill founded, has been more important in the life of man than the germ theory of decay, however true the latter may be (Joseph Wood Krutch, *The Modern Temper,* New York, 1929, p. 49).

Only the power of symbolic reference can express human values; but the facts with which science deals are not capable of symbolic reference. Primitive man's experience of the sun was of an inaccessible source of infinite light, a perfectly adequate symbol of the transcendence of God. The scientist knows the sun as a thing, a giant thermo-nuclear furnace which transforms hydrogen into helium, and he naively accuses the so-called primitive of deifying a phenomenon of nature. Because the scientific reality is not useful as a symbol there is no reason to deny the reality of the symbolic experience itself or of the experience it signifies, the intuition of God's transcendence. The man was not worshipping the thermo-nuclear furnace of which he was ignorant, he was worshipping the God he knew.

The sacral mentality in which man is alienated and becomes the passive plaything of a capricious God is already a misreading of the reality to which symbolism appeals. However, the characteristic occupational hazard of those who love symbolism is magic, which is a technique by which man hopes to control the forces of nature through the manipulation and manufacture of symbols. This secularist attitude to symbolism is as reprehensible as the sacralist attitude, and it paves the way for an improved technology which dispenses with symbolism altogether. Symbolism is not a substitute for technology, nor is it to be confused with the sacral mentality. It is the only way we have of referring to our experience of a reality that is both sacred and secular. If we reject symbolism, we reject the sacred, the human, and we end up in the contradictory proposition that 'God is dead'.

The modern, western world is secularist and obstinately refuses to see anything more than half of reality. This is because its orientation is towards the manipulation of material things, mechanical ingenuity. The last two centuries have witnessed an acceleration of scientific inventions because human mental energy has suddenly been diverted into a new channel. Why were there no inventions in earlier ages? Not because of an invincible ignorance. People could have made the discoveries if they had been looking for them, but it so happened that mechanical ingenuity did not stand very high in their scale of priorities. Their ideal of civilization was not that of the comforts of bourgeois living. Today it is, – so much so that the comfortable life of a minority based on the exploitation of cheap labour is dubbed 'white civilization' in those countries were racial discrimination is practised in order to safeguard and perpetuate it.

Humanity cannot, in fact, exist without symbolism, but men can refuse to recognize the fact. They can insist on impoverishing symbols by translating them into scientific or technical terms. They can demythologize to their heart's content. Psychologists and sociologists can analyse symbols and demonstrate their effectiveness in contributing to social and psychological equilibrium; philosophers can point to symbolization as an important ingredient of perception and communication. But ultimately symbolization is an art and not a science. It has to be practised. Western man is content to know his symbols through a poetry and a literature which create an illusion of belief, but which do not touch the fibres of his being. He is living in a sub-human, sub-cultural world disorientated by rapid social and technological change. Technology is a poor substitute for the symbols of a fully integrated human culture, in which human life has a purpose and a meaning.

Instinctively the youth of the western world have sensed

the spiritual and moral bankruptcy of society, have become 'drop-outs', have turned to the Orient and to the Negro world for new values, have tended to stress more and more the use of symbolism in human communication. They have also, too often, sensed their own powerlessness to change the established order, and have realized that dropping-out and permissiveness are not ultimately permanent or positive values. The western world is before an *impasse.* Without God, it lacks a guide for conduct; it is a world without love. Yet the secular theologian's attempt to speak of God in secular terms is doomed to failure as long as the secular excludes the notion of God by very definition, and the only possible means of speaking about him.

In this situation the 'Third World' of Africa and Asia may have a contribution to make, and the mission of the Church could be the vehicle of that contribution. The mission has to be seen as a two-way process, an essay in human communications. The ideals and values of Christianity have to be expressed in the categories and thought-patterns of non-western cultures, and this process, in turn, brings an enrichment of insights and applications to the common patrimony of Christians. Too often, alas, there has been little or no communication. Missionaries have brought a pre-fabricated Christianity and have not bothered to find out if and how it was being understood by the people they were teaching. Even, today, when so much is being said and written about the adaptation of rites, little is done about the more fundamental adaptation of the message, or to obey the injunction of the Second Vatican Council 'to stir up a theological investigation' in these cultures. This situation has encouraged the African and Asian Christian to belong to two worlds, and has prevented him from putting them together. The agnostic Ugandan poet, Okot p'Bitek has satirized the missionaries unmercifully for this failure to communicate:

> The things they shout I do not understand,
> They shout anyhow,
> They shout like mad people.
> The padre shouts words
> You cannot understand,
> And he does not seem
> To care in the least
> Whether his hearers
> Understand him or not.
> A strange language they speak
> These Christian diviner-priests,

And the white nuns
Think the girls understand
What they are saying,
And are annoyed
When they laugh
(Okot p'Bitek: *The Song of Lawino,* Nairobi, 1968, p. 116).

The failure to communicate, on the part of missionaries, and their lack of appreciation of symbolism can contribute towards the creation of a secularist mentality. This can happen without the experience of technological change – merely through inadequate missionary action. There are several well attested instances of African tribes that have lost all interest in religion since the preaching of the Christian gospel began. Before the coming of the mission to their country they were the most religious of people. Since the missionaries came, they have learned to see religion as something separate from their own way of life, something they did not perfectly understand. Their own material preoccupations continued to interest them, but the religion which replaced their traditional beliefs did not seem to have any relevance for their material life. Fortunately, such a disaster has not been common, but it is everywhere a real danger, if no real gospel penetration takes place.

The missionary ideal is one in which there is successful communication between cultures, and it implies a readiness on the part of the missionary to take the other culture seriously, to study its values systematically and – in the case of Africa and Asia – to attune his mind to the favoured symbolical forms of expression. This is not, as some African and Asian writers have maintained, a cynical take-over bid of African and Asian culture by Christianity. The Christian mission is not a take-over bid. It is the recognition that Christian and non-Christian cultures are influencing each other, and is the attempt to establish real communication and mutual enrichment. The vital question is: 'Will the Third World succumb to the secularist fallacy, or will it, through its traditional attachment to symbols, make a contribution to the rediscovery of life's meaning in a technological age?' Christianity could fertilize and stimulate the non-Christian traditions, so that such a contribution could be made. It is clearly the hope of political theorists like Nyerere, Kaunda and Senghor, that Africa will make a contribution to the development of mankind through her witness to human values and a fully integrated and meaningful life. Africa is not preaching the class-struggle but the value of human brotherhood and co-operation.

If such a contribution is made, then the Church's mission will be plainly justified in the eyes of all. The mission exists for human reconciliation and development, and this cannot be a one-sided process. Those who are evangelized are evangelized in order to become missionaries themselves, but as Fr Greeley has written:

> The size of the task is staggering. To harmonize the city and nature, the technical and the numinous, the profane and the religious is never easy (A. Greeley: *Strangers in the House,* New York, 1967, p. 72).

We are engaged in nothing less than the building of a new cosmos, a cosmos in which all things are restored – restored, as Christians believe, in Christ.

BIBLIOGRAPHY

Abbott, W. M., S.J. *The Documents of Vatican II,* London 1966 (Especially *Ad Gentes, Gaudium et Spes* and *Nostra Aetate).*

Allen, Roland. *Missionary Principles,* London 1964.

Anderson, G. H. (ed.) *Christian Mission in Theological Perspective. An Enquiry by Methodists,* Nashville New York 1967.

Beetham, T. A. *Christianity and the New Africa,* London 1967.

Beyerhaus P. and Hallencreutz C. F. (ed.) *The Church Crossing Frontiers,* Uppsala 1969.

Considine, J. J. *The Missionary's Role in Socio-Economic Betterment,* New York 1960.

Flannery A., O.P. *Missions and Religions,* Dublin 1968.

Fuller, R. H. and Rice, B. K. *Christianity and the Affluent Society,* London 1966.

Goodall, N. *Christian Missions and Social Ferment,* London 1964.

Grassi, J. M. M.M. *A World to Win. The Missionary Methods of Paul the Apostle,* Maryknoll New York 1965.

Greeley, A. *Strangers in the House,* New York 1967.

Hastings, A. *The World Mission of the Church,* London 1964.

Hastings, A. *Church and Mission in Modern Africa,* London 1967.

Hatton, D. J., Mgr. *Missiology in Africa Today,* Dublin 1961.

Hillman, E. *The Church as Mission,* London 1966.

Hillman, E. *The Wider Ecumenism,* London 1968.

Intervarsity Missionary Convention *God's Men from All Nations to All Nations,* Chicago 1968.

Jenkins D., Canon *The Glory of Man,* London 1967.

Krutch, J.W. *The Modern Temper,* New York 1929.

McCody, J., S.M. *Advice from the Field. Towards a New Missiology,* Baltimore 1962.

McGavran, D.A. (ed.) *Church Growth and Christian Mission,* New York 1965.

National Missionary Study Week, Navan, Ireland. *The Church is Mission,* London 1969.
Neill, S., Bishop *A History of Christian Missions,* Pelican Books, Harmondsworth 1964.
Neuner, J., S.J. (ed.) *Christian Revelation and World Religions,* London 1967.
Nyerere, J. K. *Ujamaa,* Oxford 1968.
Orchard, R. K. *Witness in Six Continents,* London 1964.
Paul VI *The Great Social Problem* (*Populorum Progressio*), C.T.S. London 1967.
Richardson, W. J., M.M. *The Church as Sign,* Maryknoll, New York 1968.
Senghor, L.S. *On African Socialism,* London 1964.
Schlette, H. R. *Towards a Theology of Religions,* London 1966.
Tanner, R. E. S. *Transition in African Beliefs,* Maryknoll New York 1967.
Teilhard de Chardin, P. *Le Milieu Divin,* London 1964.
Warren, M. *Social History and Christian Mission,* London 1967.
Wieser, T. *Planning for Mission,* London 1966.

INDEX

First published in The Netherlands
Made and printed by Van Boekhoven-Bosch nv, Utrecht

THEOLOGY TODAY SERIES

THE TITLES PUBLISHED TO DATE ARE:

1. The Theology of the Incarnation	*Ralph Woodhall, S.J.*
2. Theology and Revelation	*Gerald O'Collins, S.J.*
3. The Theology of Faith	*John Coventry, S.J.*
4. The Theology of the Trinity	*Laurence Cantwell, S.J.*
5. The Theology of Creation	*Robert Butterworth, S.J.*
7. The Theology of History	*Osmund Lewry, O.P.*
8. The Theology of the Church	*Peter Hebblethwaite, S.J.*
9. Theology of Ecumenism	*Michael Hurley, S.J.*
10. The Theology of Inspiration	*John Scullion, S.J.*
11. The Theology of Tradition	*Anthony Meredith, S.J.*
12. The Theology of the Word of God	*Aloysius Church, S.J.*
16. The Theology in St Paul	*Henry Wansbrough, O.S.B.*
18. Theology and Spirituality	*John Dalrymple*
21. The Christian Social Conscience	*Rodger Charles, S.J.*
25. The Theology of Baptism	*Lorna Brockett, R.S.C.J.*
28. The Theology of Original Sin	*Edward Yarnold, S.J.*
31. The Theology of Marriage	*Rosemary Haughton*
42. Death and Eternal Life	*Michael Simpson, S.J.*

FORTHCOMING TITLES

OCTOBER, 1972.

6 The Theology of Evolution by Ervin Nemesszeghy, S.J. and John Russell, S.J.

26 The Theology of Confirmation by Austin P. Milner, O.P.

NOVEMBER, 1972.

13 The Theology of God by Andrew Lascaris, O.P.

36 The Theology of Angels and Devils by Rob van der Hart, O.P.

FEBRUARY, 1973.

15 Why were the Gospels Written? by John Ashton, S.J.

33 The Priest as Preacher by Edward P. Echlin, S.J.

MARCH, 1973.

27 Theology of the Eucharist by James Quinn, S.J.

43 The Church and the World by Rodger Charles, S.J.

44 Roman Catholicism, Christianity and Anonymous Christianity by J. P. Kenny, S.J.